T&P BOOKS

# DICTIONARY

## THEME-BASED

British English Collection

# ENGLISH
# ARABIC

The most useful words
To expand your lexicon and sharpen
your language skills

**3000 words**

**Theme-based dictionary British English-Egyptian Arabic - 3000 words**
By Andrey Taranov

T&P Books vocabularies are intended for helping you learn, memorize and review foreign words. The dictionary is divided into themes, covering all major spheres of everyday activities, business, science, culture, etc.

The process of learning words using T&P Books' theme-based dictionaries gives you the following advantages:

- Correctly grouped source information predetermines success at subsequent stages of word memorization
- Availability of words derived from the same root allowing memorization of word units (rather than separate words)
- Small units of words facilitate the process of establishing associative links needed for consolidation of vocabulary
- Level of language knowledge can be estimated by the number of learned words



T&P Books Publishing
www.tpbooks.com

This book is also available in E-book formats.
Please visit www.tpbooks.com or the major online bookstores.

# EGYPTIAN ARABIC THEME-BASED DICTIONARY
## British English collection

T&P Books vocabularies are intended to help you learn, memorize, and review foreign words. The vocabulary contains over 3000 commonly used words arranged thematically.

- Vocabulary contains the most commonly used words
- Recommended as an addition to any language course
- Meets the needs of beginners and advanced learners of foreign languages
- Convenient for daily use, revision sessions, and self-testing activities
- Allows you to assess your vocabulary

**Special features of the vocabulary**

- Words are organized according to their meaning, not alphabetically
- Words are presented in three columns to facilitate the reviewing and self-testing processes
- Words in groups are divided into small blocks to facilitate the learning process
- The vocabulary offers a convenient and simple transcription of each foreign word

**The vocabulary has 101 topics including:**

Basic Concepts, Numbers, Colors, Months, Seasons, Units of Measurement, Clothing & Accessories, Food & Nutrition, Restaurant, Family Members, Relatives, Character, Feelings, Emotions, Diseases, City, Town, Sightseeing, Shopping, Money, House, Home, Office, Working in the Office, Import & Export, Marketing, Job Search, Sports, Education, Computer, Internet, Tools, Nature, Countries, Nationalities and more ...

# TABLE OF CONTENTS

# PRONUNCIATION GUIDE

| T&P phonetic alphabet | Egyptian Arabic example | English example |
|---|---|---|
| [a] | [ṭaffa] طفّى | shorter than in 'ask' |
| [ā] | [eχtār] إختار | calf, palm |
| [e] | [setta] ستّة | elm, medal |
| [i] | [minā'] ميناء | shorter than in 'feet' |
| [ī] | [ebrīl] إبريل | feet, meter |
| [o] | [oɣosṭos] أغسطس | pod, John |
| [ō] | [ḥalazōn] حلزون | fall, bomb |
| [u] | [kalkutta] كلكتا | book |
| [ū] | [gamūs] جاموس | fuel, tuna |
| | | |
| [b] | [bedāya] بداية | baby, book |
| [d] | [sa'āda] سعادة | day, doctor |
| [ḍ] | [waḍ'] وضع | [d] pharyngeal |
| [ʒ] | [arʒantīn] الأرجنتين | forge, pleasure |
| [ẓ] | [ẓahar] ظهر | [z] pharyngeal |
| [f] | [χafīf] خفيف | face, food |
| [g] | [bahga] بهجة | game, gold |
| [h] | [ettegāh] إتّجاه | home, have |
| [ḥ] | [ḥabb] حبّ | [h] pharyngeal |
| [y] | [dahaby] ذهبي | yes, New York |
| [k] | [korsy] كرسي | clock, kiss |
| [l] | [lammaḥ] لمّح | lace, people |
| [m] | [marṣad] مرصد | magic, milk |
| [n] | [ganūb] جنوب | sang, thing |
| [p] | [kaputʃino] كابتشينو | pencil, private |
| [q] | [wasaq] وثق | king, club |
| [r] | [roḥe] روح | rice, radio |
| [s] | [soχreya] سخرية | city, boss |
| [ṣ] | [me'ṣam] معصم | [s] pharyngeal |
| [ʃ] | ['aʃā'] عشاء | machine, shark |
| [t] | [tanūb] تنوب | tourist, trip |
| [ṭ] | [χarīṭa] خريطة | [t] pharyngeal |
| [θ] | [mamūθ] ماموث | month, tooth |
| [v] | [vietnām] فيتنام | very, river |
| [w] | [wadda'] ودّع | vase, winter |
| [χ] | [baχīl] بخيل | as in Scots 'loch' |

| T&P phonetic alphabet | Egyptian Arabic example | English example |
| --- | --- | --- |
| [ɣ] | **[etɣadda] إتغدّى** | between [g] and [h] |
| [z] | **[me'za] معزة** | zebra, please |
| ['] (ayn) | **[sab'a] سبعة** | voiced pharyngeal fricative |
| ['] (hamza) | **[sa'al] سأل** | glottal stop |

# ABBREVIATIONS
# used in the dictionary

## Egyptian Arabic abbreviations

| | | |
|---|---|---|
| **du** | - | plural noun (double) |
| **f** | - | feminine noun |
| **m** | - | masculine noun |
| **pl** | - | plural |

## English abbreviations

| | | |
|---|---|---|
| **ab.** | - | about |
| **adj** | - | adjective |
| **adv** | - | adverb |
| **anim.** | - | animate |
| **as adj** | - | attributive noun used as adjective |
| **e.g.** | - | for example |
| **etc.** | - | et cetera |
| **fam.** | - | familiar |
| **fem.** | - | feminine |
| **form.** | - | formal |
| **inanim.** | - | inanimate |
| **masc.** | - | masculine |
| **math** | - | mathematics |
| **mil.** | - | military |
| **n** | - | noun |
| **pl** | - | plural |
| **pron.** | - | pronoun |
| **sb** | - | somebody |
| **sing.** | - | singular |
| **sth** | - | something |
| **v aux** | - | auxiliary verb |
| **vi** | - | intransitive verb |
| **vi, vt** | - | intransitive, transitive verb |
| **vt** | - | transitive verb |

# BASIC CONCEPTS

## 1. Pronouns

| | | |
|---|---|---|
| I, me | ana | أنا |
| you (masc.) | enta | أنت |
| you (fem.) | enty | أنت |
| he | howwa | هوّ |
| she | hiya | هيّ |
| we | eḥna | إحنا |
| you (to a group) | antom | أنتم |
| they | hamm | همّ |

## 2. Greetings. Salutations

| | | |
|---|---|---|
| Hello! (form.) | assalamu ʿalaykum! | السلام عليكم! |
| Good morning! | ṣabāḥ el χeyr! | صباح الخير! |
| Good afternoon! | neharak saʿīd! | نهارك سعيد! |
| Good evening! | masāʾ el χeyr! | مساء الخير! |
| to say hello | sallem | سلّم |
| Hi! (hello) | ahlan! | أهلاً! |
| greeting (n) | salām (m) | سلام |
| to greet (vt) | sallem ʿala | سلّم على |
| How are you? | ezzayek? | ازّيك؟ |
| What's new? | aχbārak eyh? | أخبارك ايه؟ |
| Bye-Bye! Goodbye! | maʿ el salāma! | مع السلامة! |
| See you soon! | aʃūfak orayeb! | أشوفك قريب! |
| Farewell! | maʿ el salāma! | مع السلامة! |
| to say goodbye | waddaʿ | ودّع |
| Cheers! | bay bay! | باي باي! |
| Thank you! Cheers! | ʃokran! | شكراً! |
| Thank you very much! | ʃokran geddan! | شكراً جداً! |
| My pleasure! | el ʿafw | العفو |
| Don't mention it! | la ʃokr ʿala wāgeb | لا شكر على واجب |
| It was nothing | el ʿafw | العفو |
| Excuse me! (fam.) | ʿan eznak! | عن إذنك! |
| Excuse me! (form.) | baʿd ezn ḥadretak! | بعد إذن حضرتك! |
| to excuse (forgive) | ʿazar | عذر |
| to apologize (vi) | eʿtazar | أعتذر |
| My apologies | ana ʾāsef | أنا آسف |
| I'm sorry! | ana ʾāsef! | أنا آسف! |

| | | |
|---|---|---|
| to forgive (vt) | ʻafa | عفا |
| please (adv) | men faḍlak | من فضلك |
| | | |
| Don't forget! | ma tensāʃ! | ما تنساش! |
| Certainly! | ṭabʻan! | طبعاً! |
| Of course not! | laʼ ṭabʻan! | لأ طبعاً! |
| Okay! (I agree) | ettafaʼna! | إتّفقنا! |
| That's enough! | kefāya! | كفاية! |

## 3. Questions

| | | |
|---|---|---|
| Who? | mīn? | مين؟ |
| What? | eyh? | ايه؟ |
| Where? (at, in) | feyn? | فين؟ |
| Where (to)? | feyn? | فين؟ |
| From where? | meneyn? | منين؟ |
| When? | emta | امتى؟ |
| Why? (What for?) | ʻaʃān eyh? | عشان ايه؟ |
| Why? (~ are you crying?) | leyh? | ليه؟ |
| | | |
| What for? | l eyh? | لـ ليه؟ |
| How? (in what way) | ezāy? | إزاي؟ |
| What? (What kind of ...?) | eyh? | ايه؟ |
| Which? | ayī? | أيّ؟ |
| | | |
| To whom? | le mīn? | لمين؟ |
| About whom? | ʻan mīn? | عن مين؟ |
| About what? | ʻan eyh? | عن ايه؟ |
| With whom? | maʻ mīn? | مع مين؟ |
| | | |
| How many? How much? | kām? | كام؟ |
| Whose? | betāʻet mīn? | بتاعت مين؟ |

## 4. Prepositions

| | | |
|---|---|---|
| with (accompanied by) | maʻ | مع |
| without | men ɣeyr | من غير |
| to (indicating direction) | ela | إلى |
| about (talking ~ ...) | ʻan | عن |
| | | |
| before (in time) | ʼabl | قبل |
| in front of ... | ʼoddām | قدّام |
| | | |
| under (beneath, below) | taḥt | تحت |
| above (over) | foʼe | فوق |
| on (atop) | ʻala | على |
| | | |
| from (off, out of) | men | من |
| of (made from) | men | من |
| | | |
| in (e.g. ~ ten minutes) | baʻd | بعد |
| over (across the top of) | men ʻala | من على |

## 5. Function words. Adverbs. Part 1

| | | |
|---|---|---|
| Where? (at, in) | feyn? | فين؟ |
| here (adv) | hena | هنا |
| there (adv) | henāk | هناك |
| somewhere (to be) | fe makānen ma | في مكان ما |
| nowhere (not in any place) | meʃ fi ayī makān | مش في أيّ مكان |
| by (near, beside) | ganb | جنب |
| by the window | ganb el ʃebbāk | جنب الشبّاك |
| Where (to)? | feyn? | فين؟ |
| here (e.g. come ~!) | hena | هنا |
| there (e.g. to go ~) | henāk | هناك |
| from here (adv) | men hena | من هنا |
| from there (adv) | men henāk | من هناك |
| close (adv) | ʾarīb | قريب |
| far (adv) | beʿīd | بعيد |
| near (e.g. ~ Paris) | ʿand | عند |
| nearby (adv) | ʾarīb | قريب |
| not far (adv) | meʃ beʿīd | مش بعيد |
| left (adj) | el ʃemāl | الشمال |
| on the left | ʿalal ʃemāl | على الشمال |
| to the left | lel ʃemāl | للشمال |
| right (adj) | el yemīn | اليمين |
| on the right | ʿalal yemīn | على اليمين |
| to the right | lel yemīn | لليمين |
| in front (adv) | ʾoddām | قدّام |
| front (as adj) | amāmy | أمامي |
| ahead (the kids ran ~) | ela el amām | إلى الأمام |
| behind (adv) | waraʾ | وراء |
| from behind | men wara | من ورّا |
| back (towards the rear) | le wara | لورّا |
| middle | wasaṭ (m) | وسط |
| in the middle | fel wasat | في الوسط |
| at the side | ʿala ganb | على جنب |
| everywhere (adv) | fe kol makān | في كل مكان |
| around (in all directions) | ḥawaleyn | حوالين |
| from inside | men gowwah | من جوّه |
| somewhere (to go) | le ʾayī makān | لأي مكان |
| straight (directly) | ʿala ṭūl | على طول |
| back (e.g. come ~) | rogūʿ | رجوع |
| from anywhere | men ayī makān | من أيّ مكان |
| from somewhere | men makānen mā | من مكان ما |

| | | |
|---|---|---|
| firstly (adv) | awwalan | أوّلاً |
| secondly (adv) | sāneyan | ثانياً |
| thirdly (adv) | sālesan | ثالثاً |
| | | |
| suddenly (adv) | fag'a | فجأة |
| at first (in the beginning) | fel bedāya | في البداية |
| for the first time | le 'awwel marra | لأوّل مرّة |
| long before ... | 'abl ... be modda ṭawīla | قبل... بمدة طويلة |
| anew (over again) | men gedīd | من جديد |
| for good (adv) | lel abad | للأبد |
| | | |
| never (adv) | abadan | أبداً |
| again (adv) | tāny | تاني |
| now (at present) | delwa'ty | دلوقتي |
| often (adv) | ketīr | كثير |
| then (adv) | wa'taha | وقتها |
| urgently (quickly) | 'ala ṭūl | على طول |
| usually (adv) | 'ādatan | عادةً |
| | | |
| by the way, ... | 'ala fekra ... | على فكرة... |
| possibly | momken | ممكن |
| probably (adv) | momken | ممكن |
| maybe (adv) | momken | ممكن |
| besides ... | bel eḍāfa ela ... | بالإضافة إلى... |
| that's why ... | 'aʃān keda | عشان كده |
| in spite of ... | bel raɣm men ... | بالرغم من... |
| thanks to ... | be faḍl ... | بفضل... |
| | | |
| what (pron.) | elly | إللي |
| that (conj.) | ennu | إنّه |
| something | ḥāga (f) | حاجة |
| anything (something) | ayī ḥāga (f) | أيّ حاجة |
| nothing | wala ḥāga | ولا حاجة |
| | | |
| who (pron.) | elly | إللي |
| someone | ḥadd | حدّ |
| somebody | ḥadd | حدّ |
| | | |
| nobody | wala ḥadd | ولا حدّ |
| nowhere (a voyage to ~) | meʃ le wala makān | مش لـ ولا مكان |
| nobody's | wala ḥadd | ولا حدّ |
| somebody's | le ḥadd | لحدّ |
| | | |
| so (I'm ~ glad) | geddan | جداً |
| also (as well) | kamān | كمان |
| too (as well) | kamān | كمان |

## 6. Function words. Adverbs. Part 2

| | | |
|---|---|---|
| Why? | leyh? | ليه؟ |
| for some reason | le sabeben ma | لسبب ما |
| because ... | 'aʃān ... | ... عشان |
| for some purpose | le hadafen mā | لهدف ما |
| and | w | و |

| | | |
|---|---|---|
| or | walla | ولّلا |
| but | bass | بسّ |
| for (e.g. ~ me) | 'aʃān | عشان |
| | | |
| too (excessively) | ketīr geddan | كتير جدّاً |
| only (exclusively) | bass | بسّ |
| exactly (adv) | bel ḍabṭ | بالضبط |
| about (more or less) | naḥw | نحو |
| | | |
| approximately (adv) | naḥw | نحو |
| approximate (adj) | taqrīby | تقريبي |
| almost (adv) | ta'rīban | تقريباً |
| the rest | el bā'y (m) | الباقي |
| | | |
| each (adj) | koll | كلّ |
| any (no matter which) | ayī | أيّ |
| many, much (a lot of) | ketīr | كتير |
| many people | nās ketīr | ناس كتير |
| all (everyone) | koll el nās | كلّ الناس |
| | | |
| in return for ... | fi moqābel ... | ... في مقابل |
| in exchange (adv) | fe moqābel | في مقابل |
| by hand (made) | bel yad | باليد |
| hardly (negative opinion) | bel kād | بالكاد |
| | | |
| probably (adv) | momken | ممكن |
| on purpose (intentionally) | bel 'aṣd | بالقصد |
| by accident (adv) | bel ṣodfa | بالصدفة |
| | | |
| very (adv) | 'awy | قوّي |
| for example (adv) | masalan | مثلاً |
| between | beyn | بين |
| among | wesṭ | وسط |
| so much (such a lot) | ketīr | كتير |
| especially (adv) | χāṣṣa | خاصّة |

# NUMBERS. MISCELLANEOUS

## 7. Cardinal numbers. Part 1

| | | |
|---|---|---|
| 0 zero | ṣefr | صفر |
| 1 one | wāḥed | واحد |
| 1 one (fem.) | waḥda | واحدة |
| 2 two | etneyn | إتنين |
| 3 three | talāta | ثلاثة |
| 4 four | arbaʿa | أربعة |
| 5 five | χamsa | خمسة |
| 6 six | setta | ستّة |
| 7 seven | sabʿa | سبعة |
| 8 eight | tamanya | ثمانية |
| 9 nine | tesʿa | تسعة |
| 10 ten | ʿaʃara | عشرة |
| 11 eleven | ḥedāʃar | حداشر |
| 12 twelve | etnāʃar | إتناشر |
| 13 thirteen | talattāʃar | تلاتّاشر |
| 14 fourteen | arbaʿtāʃer | أربعتاشر |
| 15 fifteen | χamastāʃer | خمستاشر |
| 16 sixteen | settāʃar | ستّاشر |
| 17 seventeen | sabaʿtāʃar | سبعتاشر |
| 18 eighteen | tamantāʃar | تمنتاشر |
| 19 nineteen | tesʿatāʃar | تسعتاشر |
| 20 twenty | ʿeʃrīn | عشرين |
| 21 twenty-one | wāḥed we ʿeʃrīn | واحد وعشرين |
| 22 twenty-two | etneyn we ʿeʃrīn | إتنين وعشرين |
| 23 twenty-three | talāta we ʿeʃrīn | ثلاثة وعشرين |
| 30 thirty | talatīn | ثلاثين |
| 31 thirty-one | wāḥed we talatīn | واحد وتلاتين |
| 32 thirty-two | etneyn we talatīn | إتنين وتلاتين |
| 33 thirty-three | talāta we talatīn | ثلاثة وثلاثين |
| 40 forty | arbeʿīn | أربعين |
| 41 forty-one | wāḥed we arbeʿīn | واحد وأربعين |
| 42 forty-two | etneyn we arbeʿīn | إتنين وأربعين |
| 43 forty-three | talāta we arbeʿīn | ثلاثة وأربعين |
| 50 fifty | χamsīn | خمسين |
| 51 fifty-one | wāḥed we χamsīn | واحد وخمسين |
| 52 fifty-two | etneyn we χamsīn | إتنين وخمسين |
| 53 fifty-three | talāta we χamsīn | ثلاثة وخمسين |
| 60 sixty | settīn | ستّين |
| 61 sixty-one | wāḥed we settīn | واحد وستّين |

| | | |
|---|---|---|
| 62 sixty-two | etneyn we settīn | إتنين وستّين |
| 63 sixty-three | talāta we settīn | ثلاثة وستّين |
| 70 seventy | sab'īn | سبعين |
| 71 seventy-one | wāḥed we sab'īn | واحد وسبعين |
| 72 seventy-two | etneyn we sab'īn | إتنين وسبعين |
| 73 seventy-three | talāta we sab'īn | ثلاثة وسبعين |
| 80 eighty | tamanīn | ثمانين |
| 81 eighty-one | wāḥed we tamanīn | واحد وتمانين |
| 82 eighty-two | etneyn we tamanīn | إتنين وتمانين |
| 83 eighty-three | talāta we tamanīn | ثلاثة وثمانين |
| 90 ninety | tes'īn | تسعين |
| 91 ninety-one | wāḥed we tes'īn | واحد وتسعين |
| 92 ninety-two | etneyn we tes'īn | إتنين وتسعين |
| 93 ninety-three | talāta we tes'īn | ثلاثة وتسعين |

## 8. Cardinal numbers. Part 2

| | | |
|---|---|---|
| 100 one hundred | miya | ميّة |
| 200 two hundred | meteyn | ميتين |
| 300 three hundred | toltomiya | تلتميّة |
| 400 four hundred | rob'omiya | ربعميّة |
| 500 five hundred | χomsomiya | خمسميّة |
| 600 six hundred | sotomiya | ستميّة |
| 700 seven hundred | sob'omiya | سبعميّة |
| 800 eight hundred | tomnome'a | ثمنمئة |
| 900 nine hundred | tos'omiya | تسعميّة |
| 1000 one thousand | alf | ألف |
| 2000 two thousand | alfeyn | ألفين |
| 3000 three thousand | talat 'ālāf | ثلاث آلاف |
| 10000 ten thousand | 'aʃaret 'ālāf | عشرة آلاف |
| one hundred thousand | mīt alf | ميت ألف |
| million | millyon (m) | مليون |
| billion | millyār (m) | مليار |

## 9. Ordinal numbers

| | | |
|---|---|---|
| first (adj) | awwel | أوّل |
| second (adj) | tāny | ثاني |
| third (adj) | tālet | ثالث |
| fourth (adj) | rābe' | رابع |
| fifth (adj) | χāmes | خامس |
| sixth (adj) | sādes | سادس |
| seventh (adj) | sābe' | سابع |
| eighth (adj) | tāmen | ثامن |
| ninth (adj) | tāse' | تاسع |
| tenth (adj) | 'āʃer | عاشر |

# COLORS. UNITS OF MEASUREMENT

## 10. Colours

| | | |
|---|---|---|
| colour | lone (m) | لون |
| shade (tint) | daraget el lōn (m) | درجة اللون |
| hue | ṣabɣet lōn (f) | صبغة اللون |
| rainbow | qose qozaḥ (m) | قوس قزح |
| white (adj) | abyaḍ | أبيض |
| black (adj) | aswad | أسود |
| grey (adj) | romādy | رمادي |
| green (adj) | aχḍar | أخضر |
| yellow (adj) | aṣfar | أصفر |
| red (adj) | aḥmar | أحمر |
| blue (adj) | azra' | أزرق |
| light blue (adj) | azra' fāteḥ | أزرق فاتح |
| pink (adj) | wardy | وردي |
| orange (adj) | bortoqāly | برتقاليّ |
| violet (adj) | banaffsegy | بنفّسجي |
| brown (adj) | bonny | بنّي |
| golden (adj) | dahaby | ذهبي |
| silvery (adj) | feḍḍy | فضّي |
| beige (adj) | bɛ:ʒ | بيج |
| cream (adj) | ʻāgy | عاجيّ |
| turquoise (adj) | fayrūzy | فيروزي |
| cherry red (adj) | aḥmar karazy | أحمر كرزي |
| lilac (adj) | laylaky | ليّلكي |
| crimson (adj) | qormozy | قرمزي |
| light (adj) | fāteḥ | فاتح |
| dark (adj) | ɣāme' | غامق |
| bright, vivid (adj) | zāhy | زاهي |
| coloured (pencils) | melawwen | ملوّن |
| colour (e.g. ~ film) | melawwen | ملوّن |
| black-and-white (adj) | abyaḍ we aswad | أبيض وأسوّد |
| plain (one-coloured) | sāda | سادة |
| multicoloured (adj) | motaʻadded el alwān | متعددّ الألوان |

## 11. Units of measurement

| | | |
|---|---|---|
| weight | wazn (m) | وزن |
| length | ṭūl (m) | طول |

| | | |
|---|---|---|
| width | ʿarḍ (m) | عرض |
| height | ertefāʿ (m) | إرتفاع |
| depth | ʿomq (m) | عمق |
| volume | ḥagm (m) | حجم |
| area | mesāḥa (f) | مساحة |
| | | |
| gram | gram (m) | جرام |
| milligram | milligrām (m) | ملّيغرام |
| kilogram | kilogrām (m) | كيلوغرام |
| ton | ṭenn (m) | طنّ |
| pound | reṭl (m) | رطل |
| ounce | onṣa (f) | أونصة |
| | | |
| metre | metr (m) | متر |
| millimetre | millimetr (m) | ملّيمتر |
| centimetre | santimetr (m) | سنتيمتر |
| kilometre | kilometr (m) | كيلومتر |
| mile | mīl (m) | ميل |
| | | |
| inch | boṣa (f) | بوصة |
| foot | ʾadam (m) | قدم |
| yard | yarda (f) | ياردة |
| | | |
| square metre | metr morabbaʿ (m) | متر مربّع |
| hectare | hektār (m) | هكتار |
| | | |
| litre | litre (m) | لتر |
| degree | daraga (f) | درجة |
| volt | volt (m) | فولت |
| ampere | ambere (m) | أمبير |
| horsepower | ḥoṣān (m) | حصان |
| | | |
| quantity | kemiya (f) | كميّة |
| a little bit of … | ʃewayet … | شويّة... |
| half | noṣṣ (m) | نصّ |
| dozen | desta (f) | دستة |
| piece (item) | waḥda (f) | وحدة |
| | | |
| size | ḥagm (m) | حجم |
| scale (map ~) | meʾyās (m) | مقياس |
| | | |
| minimal (adj) | el adna | الأدنى |
| the smallest (adj) | el aṣɣar | الأصغر |
| medium (adj) | motawasseṭ | متوّسط |
| maximal (adj) | el aqṣa | الأقصى |
| the largest (adj) | el akbar | الأكبر |

## 12. Containers

| | | |
|---|---|---|
| canning jar (glass ~) | barṭamān (m) | برطمان |
| tin, can | kanz (m) | كانز |
| bucket | gardal (m) | جردل |
| barrel | barmīl (m) | برميل |
| wash basin (e.g., plastic ~) | ḥoḍe lel ɣasīl (m) | حوض للغسيل |

| | | |
|---|---|---|
| tank (100L water ~) | χazzān (m) | خزّان |
| hip flask | zamzamiya (f) | زمزميّة |
| jerrycan | ʒerken (m) | جركن |
| tank (e.g., tank car) | χazzān (m) | خزّان |
| | | |
| mug | mugg (m) | ماجّ |
| cup (of coffee, etc.) | fengān (m) | فنجان |
| saucer | ṭaba' fengān (m) | طبق فنجان |
| glass (tumbler) | kobbāya (f) | كوبّاية |
| wine glass | kāsa (f) | كاسة |
| stock pot (soup pot) | ḥalla (f) | حلّة |
| | | |
| bottle (~ of wine) | ezāza (f) | إزازة |
| neck (of the bottle, etc.) | 'onq (m) | عنق |
| | | |
| carafe (decanter) | dawra' zogāgy (m) | دوّرق زجاجي |
| pitcher | ebrī' (m) | إبريق |
| vessel (container) | we'ā' (m) | وعاء |
| pot (crock, stoneware ~) | aṣīṣ (m) | أصيص |
| vase | vāza (f) | فازة |
| | | |
| flacon, bottle (perfume ~) | ezāza (f) | إزازة |
| vial, small bottle | ezāza (f) | إزازة |
| tube (of toothpaste) | anbūba (f) | أنبوبة |
| | | |
| sack (bag) | kīs (m) | كيس |
| bag (paper ~, plastic ~) | kīs (m) | كيس |
| packet (of cigarettes, etc.) | 'elba (f) | علبة |
| | | |
| box (e.g. shoebox) | 'elba (f) | علبة |
| crate | ṣandū' (m) | صندوق |
| basket | salla (f) | سلّة |

# MAIN VERBS

## 13. The most important verbs. Part 1

| | | |
|---|---|---|
| to advise (vt) | naṣaḥ | نصح |
| to agree (say yes) | ettafa' | إتّفق |
| to answer (vi, vt) | gāwab | جاوب |
| to apologize (vi) | e'tazar | إعتذر |
| to arrive (vi) | weṣel | وصل |
| to ask (~ oneself) | sa'al | سأل |
| to ask (~ sb to do sth) | ṭalab | طلب |
| to be (vi) | kān | كان |
| to be afraid | χāf | خاف |
| to be hungry | 'āyez 'ākol | عايز آكل |
| to be interested in … | ehtamm be | إهتمّ بـ |
| to be needed | maṭlūb | مطلوب |
| to be surprised | etfāge' | إتفاجئ |
| to be thirsty | 'āyez aʃrab | عايز أشرب |
| to begin (vt) | bada' | بدأ |
| to belong to … | χaṣṣ | خصّ |
| to boast (vi) | tabāha | تباهى |
| to break (split into pieces) | kasar | كسر |
| to call (~ for help) | estaɣās | إستغاث |
| can (v aux) | 'eder | قدر |
| to catch (vt) | mesek | مسك |
| to change (vt) | ɣayar | غيّر |
| to choose (select) | eχtār | إختار |
| to come down (the stairs) | nezel | نزل |
| to compare (vt) | qāran | قارن |
| to complain (vi, vt) | ʃaka | شكا |
| to confuse (mix up) | etlaχbaṭ | إتلخبط |
| to continue (vt) | wāṣel | واصل |
| to control (vt) | et-ḥakkem | إتحكّم |
| to cook (dinner) | ḥaḍḍar | حضّر |
| to cost (vt) | kallef | كلّف |
| to count (add up) | 'add | عدّ |
| to count on … | e'tamad 'ala … | إعتمد على... |
| to create (vt) | 'amal | عمل |
| to cry (weep) | baka | بكى |

## 14. The most important verbs. Part 2

| | | |
|---|---|---|
| to deceive (vi, vt) | χada' | خدع |
| to decorate (tree, street) | zayen | زيّن |

| | | |
|---|---|---|
| to defend (a country, etc.) | dāfaʿ | دافع |
| to demand (request firmly) | ṭāleb | طالب |
| to dig (vt) | ḥafar | حفر |
| to discuss (vt) | nā'eʃ | ناقش |
| to do (vt) | ʿamal | عمل |
| to doubt (have doubts) | ʃakk fe | شكّ في |
| to drop (let fall) | wa''aʿ | وقّع |
| to enter (room, house, etc.) | daχal | دخل |
| to exist (vi) | kān mawgūd | كان موّجود |
| to expect (foresee) | tanabbaʾ | تنبّأ |
| to explain (vt) | ʃaraḥ | شرح |
| to fall (vi) | we'eʿ | وقع |
| to fancy (vt) | ʿagab | عجب |
| to find (vt) | la'a | لقي |
| to finish (vt) | χallaṣ | خلّص |
| to fly (vi) | ṭār | طار |
| to follow ... (come after) | tatabbaʿ | تتبّع |
| to forget (vi, vt) | nesy | نسي |
| to forgive (vt) | ʿafa | عفا |
| to give (vt) | edda | إدّى |
| to give a hint | edda lamḥa | إدّى لمحة |
| to go (on foot) | meʃy | مشى |
| to go for a swim | sebeḥ | سبح |
| to go out (for dinner, etc.) | χarag | خرج |
| to guess (the answer) | χammen | خمن |
| to have (vt) | malak | ملك |
| to have breakfast | feṭer | فطر |
| to have dinner | etʿasʃa | إتعشّى |
| to have lunch | etɣadda | إتغدّى |
| to hear (vt) | semeʿ | سمع |
| to help (vt) | sāʿed | ساعد |
| to hide (vt) | χabba | خبّأ |
| to hope (vi, vt) | tamanna | تمنّى |
| to hunt (vi, vt) | eṣṭād | اصطاد |
| to hurry (vi) | estaʿgel | إستعجل |

## 15. The most important verbs. Part 3

| | | |
|---|---|---|
| to inform (vt) | 'āl ly | قال لي |
| to insist (vi, vt) | aṣarr | أصرّ |
| to insult (vt) | ahān | أهان |
| to invite (vt) | ʿazam | عزم |
| to joke (vi) | hazzar | هزّر |
| to keep (vt) | ḥafaẓ | حفظ |
| to keep silent, to hush | seket | سكت |
| to kill (vt) | 'atal | قتل |

| | | |
|---|---|---|
| to know (sb) | ʿeref | عرف |
| to know (sth) | ʿeref | عرف |
| to laugh (vi) | ḍeḥek | ضحك |
| to liberate (city, etc.) | ḥarrar | حرّر |
| to look for ... (search) | dawwar ʿala | دوِّر على |
| to love (sb) | ḥabb | حبّ |
| to make a mistake | ɣeleṭ | غلط |
| to manage, to run | adār | أدار |
| to mean (signify) | ʾaṣad | قصد |
| to mention (talk about) | zakar | ذكر |
| to miss (school, etc.) | ɣāb | غاب |
| to notice (see) | lāḥaẓ | لاحظ |
| to object (vi, vt) | eʿtaraḍ | إعترض |
| to observe (see) | rāqab | راقب |
| to open (vt) | fataḥ | فتح |
| to order (meal, etc.) | ṭalab | طلب |
| to order (mil.) | amar | أمر |
| to own (possess) | malak | ملك |
| to participate (vi) | ʃārek | شارك |
| to pay (vi, vt) | dafaʿ | دفع |
| to permit (vt) | samaḥ | سمح |
| to plan (vt) | χaṭṭeṭ | خطّط |
| to play (children) | leʿeb | لعب |
| to pray (vi, vt) | ṣalla | صلّى |
| to prefer (vt) | faḍḍal | فضّل |
| to promise (vt) | waʿad | وعد |
| to pronounce (vt) | naṭaʾ | نطق |
| to propose (vt) | ʿaraḍ | عرض |
| to punish (vt) | ʿāqab | عاقب |

## 16. The most important verbs. Part 4

| | | |
|---|---|---|
| to read (vi, vt) | ʾara | قرأ |
| to recommend (vt) | naṣaḥ | نصح |
| to refuse (vi, vt) | rafaḍ | رفض |
| to regret (be sorry) | nedem | ندم |
| to rent (sth from sb) | estʾgar | إستأجر |
| to repeat (say again) | karrar | كرّر |
| to reserve, to book | ḥagaz | حجز |
| to run (vi) | gery | جري |
| to save (rescue) | anqaz | أنقذ |
| to say (~ thank you) | ʾāl | قال |
| to scold (vt) | wabbeχ | وبّخ |
| to see (vt) | ʃāf | شاف |
| to sell (vt) | bāʿ | باع |
| to send (vt) | arsal | أرسل |
| to shoot (vi) | ḍarab bel nār | ضرب بالنار |

| | | |
|---|---|---|
| to shout (vi) | ṣarraχ | صرّخ |
| to show (vt) | warra | ورّى |
| to sign (document) | waqqaʿ | وقّع |
| to sit down (vi) | ʾaʿad | قعد |
| to smile (vi) | ebtasam | إبتسم |
| to speak (vi, vt) | kallem | كلّم |
| to steal (money, etc.) | saraʾ | سرق |
| to stop (for pause, etc.) | waʾʾaf | وقّف |
| to stop (please ~ calling me) | baṭṭal | بطّل |
| to study (vt) | daras | درس |
| to swim (vi) | ʿām | عام |
| to take (vt) | aχad | أخد |
| to think (vi, vt) | fakkar | فكّر |
| to threaten (vt) | hadded | هدّد |
| to touch (with hands) | lamas | لمس |
| to translate (vt) | targem | ترجم |
| to trust (vt) | wasaq | وثق |
| to try (attempt) | ḥāwel | حاول |
| to turn (e.g., ~ left) | ḥād | حاد |
| to underestimate (vt) | estaχaff | إستخفّ |
| to understand (vt) | fehem | فهم |
| to unite (vt) | waḥḥed | وحّد |
| to wait (vt) | estanna | إستنّى |
| to want (wish, desire) | ʿāyez | عايز |
| to warn (vt) | ḥazzar | حذّر |
| to work (vi) | eʃtaɣal | إشتغل |
| to write (vt) | katab | كتب |
| to write down | katab | كتب |

# TIME. CALENDAR

## 17. Weekdays

| | | |
|---|---|---|
| Monday | el etneyn (m) | الإتنين |
| Tuesday | el talāt (m) | التلات |
| Wednesday | el arbe'ā' (m) | الأربعاء |
| Thursday | el χamīs (m) | الخميس |
| Friday | el gom'a (m) | الجمعة |
| Saturday | el sabt (m) | السبت |
| Sunday | el aḥad (m) | الأحد |
| | | |
| today (adv) | el naharda | النهارده |
| tomorrow (adv) | bokra | بكرة |
| the day after tomorrow | ba'd bokra (m) | بعد بكرة |
| yesterday (adv) | embāreḥ | امبارح |
| the day before yesterday | awwel embāreḥ | أوّل امبارح |
| | | |
| day | yome (m) | يوم |
| working day | yome 'amal (m) | يوم عمل |
| public holiday | agāza rasmiya (f) | أجازة رسميّة |
| day off | yome el agāza (m) | يوم أجازة |
| weekend | nehāyet el osbū' (f) | نهاية الأسبوع |
| | | |
| all day long | ṭūl el yome | طول اليوم |
| the next day (adv) | fel yome elly ba'dīh | في اليوم اللي بعديه |
| two days ago | men yomeyn | من يومين |
| the day before | fel yome elly 'ablo | في اليوم اللي قبله |
| daily (adj) | yawmy | يومي |
| every day (adv) | yawmiyan | يومياً |
| | | |
| week | osbū' (m) | أسبوع |
| last week (adv) | el esbū' elly fāt | الأسبوع اللي فات |
| next week (adv) | el esbū' elly gayī | الأسبوع اللي جاي |
| weekly (adj) | osbū'y | أسبوعي |
| every week (adv) | osbū'iyan | أسبوعياً |
| twice a week | marreteyn fel osbū' | مرّتين في الأسبوع |
| every Tuesday | koll solasā' | كلّ ثلاثاء |

## 18. Hours. Day and night

| | | |
|---|---|---|
| morning | ṣobḥ (m) | صبح |
| in the morning | fel ṣobḥ | في الصبح |
| noon, midday | ẓohr (m) | ظهر |
| in the afternoon | ba'd el ḍohr | بعد الظهر |
| | | |
| evening | leyl (m) | ليل |
| in the evening | bel leyl | بالليل |

| | | |
|---|---|---|
| night | leyl (m) | ليل |
| at night | bel leyl | بالليل |
| midnight | noṣṣ el leyl (m) | نصّ الليل |
| | | |
| second | sanya (f) | ثانية |
| minute | deʾīʾa (f) | دقيقة |
| hour | sāʿa (f) | ساعة |
| half an hour | noṣṣ sāʿa (m) | نصّ ساعة |
| a quarter-hour | robʿ sāʿa (f) | ربع ساعة |
| fifteen minutes | χamastāʃer deʾīʾa | خمستاشر دقيقة |
| 24 hours | arbaʿa we ʿeʃrīn sāʿa | أربعة وعشرين ساعة |
| | | |
| sunrise | ʃorūʾ el ʃams (m) | شروق الشمس |
| dawn | fagr (m) | فجر |
| early morning | ṣobḥ badry (m) | صبح بدري |
| sunset | ɣorūb el ʃams (m) | غروب الشمس |
| | | |
| early in the morning | el ṣobḥ badry | الصبح بدري |
| this morning | el naharda el ṣobḥ | النهاردة الصبح |
| tomorrow morning | bokra el ṣobḥ | بكرة الصبح |
| | | |
| this afternoon | el naharda baʿd el ḍohr | النهاردة بعد الظهر |
| in the afternoon | baʿd el ḍohr | بعد الظهر |
| tomorrow afternoon | bokra baʿd el ḍohr | بكرة بعد الظهر |
| | | |
| tonight (this evening) | el naharda bel leyl | النهاردة بالليل |
| tomorrow night | bokra bel leyl | بكرة بالليل |
| | | |
| at 3 o'clock sharp | es sāʿa talāta bel ḍabṭ | الساعة تلاتة بالضبط |
| about 4 o'clock | es sāʿa arbaʿa taʾrīban | الساعة أربعة تقريبا |
| by 12 o'clock | ḥatt es sāʿa etnāʃar | حتى الساعة إتناشر |
| in 20 minutes | fe χelāl ʿeʃrīn deʿeeʿa | في خلال عشرين دقيقة |
| in an hour | fe χelāl sāʿa | في خلال ساعة |
| on time (adv) | fe mawʿedo | في موعده |
| | | |
| a quarter to … | ella robʿ | إلّا ربع |
| within an hour | χelāl sāʿa | خلال ساعة |
| every 15 minutes | koll robʿ sāʿa | كلّ ربع ساعة |
| round the clock | leyl nahār | ليل نهار |

## 19. Months. Seasons

| | | |
|---|---|---|
| January | yanāyer (m) | يناير |
| February | febrāyer (m) | فبراير |
| March | māres (m) | مارس |
| April | ebrīl (m) | إبريل |
| May | māyo (m) | مايو |
| June | yonyo (m) | يونيو |
| | | |
| July | yolyo (m) | يوليو |
| August | oɣosṭos (m) | أغسطس |
| September | sebtamber (m) | سبتمبر |
| October | oktober (m) | أكتوبر |
| November | november (m) | نوفمبر |

| | | |
|---|---|---|
| December | desember (m) | ديسمبر |
| spring | rabee' (m) | ربيع |
| in spring | fel rabee' | في الربيع |
| spring (as adj) | rabee'y | ربيعي |
| | | |
| summer | ṣeyf (m) | صيف |
| in summer | fel ṣeyf | في الصيف |
| summer (as adj) | ṣeyfy | صيفي |
| | | |
| autumn | χarīf (m) | خريف |
| in autumn | fel χarīf | في الخريف |
| autumn (as adj) | χarīfy | خريفي |
| | | |
| winter | ʃetā' (m) | شتاء |
| in winter | fel ʃetā' | في الشتاء |
| winter (as adj) | ʃetwy | شتوّي |
| | | |
| month | ʃahr (m) | شهر |
| this month | fel ʃahr da | في الشهر ده |
| next month | el ʃahr el gayī | الشهر الجايّ |
| last month | el ʃahr elly fāt | الشهر اللي فات |
| a month ago | men ʃahr | من شهر |
| in a month (a month later) | ba'd ʃahr | بعد شهر |
| in 2 months (2 months later) | ba'd ʃahreyn | بعد شهرين |
| the whole month | el ʃahr kollo | الشهر كلّه |
| all month long | ṭawāl el ʃahr | طوال الشهر |
| | | |
| monthly (~ magazine) | ʃahry | شهري |
| monthly (adv) | ʃahry | شهري |
| every month | koll ʃahr | كلّ شهر |
| twice a month | marreteyn fel ʃahr | مرّتين في الشهر |
| | | |
| year | sana (f) | سنة |
| this year | el sana di | السنة دي |
| next year | el sana el gaya | السنة الجايّة |
| last year | el sana elly fātet | السنة اللي فاتت |
| | | |
| a year ago | men sana | من سنة |
| in a year | ba'd sana | بعد سنة |
| in two years | ba'd sanateyn | بعد سنتين |
| the whole year | el sana kollaha | السنة كلّها |
| all year long | ṭūl el sana | طول السنة |
| | | |
| every year | koll sana | كلّ سنة |
| annual (adj) | sanawy | سنوّي |
| annually (adv) | koll sana | كلّ سنة |
| 4 times a year | arba' marrāt fel sana | أربع مرات في السنة |
| | | |
| date (e.g. today's ~) | tarīχ (m) | تاريخ |
| date (e.g. ~ of birth) | tarīχ (m) | تاريخ |
| calendar | natīga (f) | نتيجة |
| | | |
| half a year | noṣṣ sana | نصّ سنة |
| six months | settet aʃ-hor (f) | ستّة أشهر |
| season (summer, etc.) | faṣl (m) | فصل |
| century | qarn (m) | قرن |

# TRAVEL. HOTEL

## 20. Trip. Travel

| | | |
|---|---|---|
| tourism, travel | seyāḥa (f) | سياحة |
| tourist | sā'eḥ (m) | سائح |
| trip, voyage | reḥla (f) | رحلة |
| adventure | moɣamra (f) | مغامرة |
| trip, journey | reḥla (f) | رحلة |
| holiday | agāza (f) | أجازة |
| to be on holiday | kān fi agāza | كان في أجازة |
| rest | estrāḥa (f) | إستراحة |
| train | qeṭār, 'aṭṭr (m) | قطار |
| by train | bel qeṭār - bel aṭṭr | بالقطار |
| aeroplane | ṭayāra (f) | طيّارة |
| by aeroplane | bel ṭayāra | بالطيّارة |
| by car | bel sayāra | بالسيّارة |
| by ship | bel safīna | بالسفينة |
| luggage | el ʃonaṭ (pl) | الشنط |
| suitcase | ʃanṭa (f) | شنطة |
| luggage trolley | 'arabet ʃonaṭ (f) | عربة شنط |
| passport | basbore (m) | باسبور |
| visa | ta'ʃīra (f) | تأشيرة |
| ticket | tazkara (f) | تذكرة |
| air ticket | tazkara ṭayarān (f) | تذكرة طيران |
| guidebook | dalīl (m) | دليل |
| map (tourist ~) | xarīṭa (f) | خريطة |
| area (rural ~) | mante'a (f) | منطقة |
| place, site | makān (m) | مكان |
| exotica (n) | ɣarāba (f) | غرابة |
| exotic (adj) | ɣarīb | غريب |
| amazing (adj) | mod-heʃ | مدهش |
| group | magmū'a (f) | مجموعة |
| excursion, sightseeing tour | gawla (f) | جولة |
| guide (person) | morʃed (m) | مرشد |

## 21. Hotel

| | | |
|---|---|---|
| hotel | fondo' (m) | فندق |
| motel | motel (m) | موتيل |
| three-star (~ hotel) | talat nogūm | ثلاث نجوم |

| | | |
|---|---|---|
| five-star | χamas nogūm | خمس نجوم |
| to stay (in a hotel, etc.) | nezel | نزل |
| room | oḍa (f) | أوضة |
| single room | owḍa le ʃaχṣ wāḥed (f) | أوضة لشخص واحد |
| double room | oḍa le ʃaχṣeyn (f) | أوضة لشخصين |
| to book a room | ḥagaz owḍa | حجز أوضة |
| half board | wagbeteyn fel yome (du) | وجبتين في اليوم |
| full board | talat wagabāt fel yome | ثلاث وجبات في اليوم |
| with bath | bel banyo | بـ البانيو |
| with shower | bel doʃ | بالدوش |
| satellite television | televizion be qanawāt faḍā'iya (m) | تليفزيون بقنوات فضائية |
| air-conditioner | takyīf (m) | تكييف |
| towel | fūṭa (f) | فوطة |
| key | meftāḥ (m) | مفتاح |
| administrator | modīr (m) | مدير |
| chambermaid | ʿāmela tandīf ɣoraf (f) | عاملة تنظيف غرف |
| porter | ʃayāl (m) | شيّال |
| doorman | bawwāb (m) | بوّاب |
| restaurant | maṭʿam (m) | مطعم |
| pub, bar | bār (m) | بار |
| breakfast | foṭūr (m) | فطور |
| dinner | ʿaʃā' (m) | عشاء |
| buffet | bofeyh (m) | بوفيه |
| lobby | rad-ha (f) | ردهة |
| lift | asanseyr (m) | اسانسير |
| DO NOT DISTURB | nargu ʿadam el ezʿāg | نرجو عدم الإزعاج |
| NO SMOKING | mamnūʿ el tadχīn | ممنوع التدخين |

## 22. Sightseeing

| | | |
|---|---|---|
| monument | temsāl (m) | تمثال |
| fortress | 'alʿa (f) | قلعة |
| palace | 'aṣr (m) | قصر |
| castle | 'alʿa (f) | قلعة |
| tower | borg (m) | برج |
| mausoleum | ḍarīḥ (m) | ضريح |
| architecture | handasa meʿmāriya (f) | هندسة معمارية |
| medieval (adj) | men el qorūn el wosṭa | من القرون الوسطى |
| ancient (adj) | ʿatīq | عتيق |
| national (adj) | waṭany | وطني |
| famous (monument, etc.) | maʃ-hūr | مشهور |
| tourist | sā'eḥ (m) | سائح |
| guide (person) | morʃed (m) | مرشد |
| excursion, sightseeing tour | gawla (f) | جولة |

| | | |
|---|---|---|
| to show (vt) | warra | ورّى |
| to tell (vt) | ʾāl | قال |
| | | |
| to find (vt) | laʾa | لقى |
| to get lost (lose one's way) | ḍāʿ | ضاع |
| map (e.g. underground ~) | χarīṭa (f) | خريطة |
| map (e.g. city ~) | χarīṭa (f) | خريطة |
| | | |
| souvenir, gift | tezkār (m) | تذكار |
| gift shop | maḥal hadāya (m) | محل هدايا |
| to take pictures | ṣawwar | صوّر |
| to have one's picture taken | etṣawwar | إتصوّر |

# TRANSPORT

## 23. Airport

| | | |
|---|---|---|
| airport | maṭār (m) | مطار |
| aeroplane | ṭayāra (f) | طيّارة |
| airline | ʃerket ṭayarān (f) | شركة طيران |
| air traffic controller | marākeb el ḥaraka el gawiya (m) | مراكب الحركة الجويّة |
| departure | moɣadra (f) | مغادرة |
| arrival | woṣūl (m) | وصول |
| to arrive (by plane) | weṣel | وصل |
| departure time | wa'ʾt el moɣadra (m) | وقت المغادرة |
| arrival time | wa'ʾt el woṣūl (m) | وقت الوصول |
| to be delayed | ta'akχar | تأخّر |
| flight delay | ta'aχor el reḥla (m) | تأخّر الرحلة |
| information board | lawḥet el maʿlomāt (f) | لوحة المعلومات |
| information | esteʿlamāt (pl) | إستعلامات |
| to announce (vt) | aʿlan | أعلن |
| flight (e.g. next ~) | reḥlet ṭayarān (f) | رحلة طيران |
| customs | gamārek (pl) | جمارك |
| customs officer | mowazzaf el gamārek (m) | موظّف الجمارك |
| customs declaration | taṣrīḥ gomroky (m) | تصريح جمركي |
| to fill in (vt) | mala | ملا |
| to fill in the declaration | mala el taṣrīḥ | ملأ التصريح |
| passport control | taftīʃ el gawazāt (m) | تفتيش الجوازات |
| luggage | el ʃonaṭ (pl) | الشنط |
| hand luggage | ʃonaṭ el yad (pl) | شنط اليد |
| luggage trolley | ʿarabet ʃonaṭ (f) | عربة شنط |
| landing | hobūṭ (m) | هبوط |
| landing strip | mamarr el hobūṭ (m) | ممرّ الهبوط |
| to land (vi) | habaṭ | هبط |
| airstair (passenger stair) | sellem el ṭayāra (m) | سلّم الطيّارة |
| check-in | tasgīl (m) | تسجيل |
| check-in counter | makān tasgīl (m) | مكان تسجيل |
| to check-in (vi) | saggel | سجّل |
| boarding card | beṭāqet el rokūb (f) | بطاقة الركوب |
| departure gate | bawwābet el moɣadra (f) | بوّابة المغادرة |
| transit | tranzīt (m) | ترانزيت |
| to wait (vt) | estanna | إستنّى |

| | | |
|---|---|---|
| departure lounge | ṣālet el moɣadra (f) | صالة المغادرة |
| to see off | wadda‘ | ودّع |
| to say goodbye | wadda‘ | ودّع |

## 24. Aeroplane

| | | |
|---|---|---|
| aeroplane | ṭayāra (f) | طيّارة |
| air ticket | tazkara ṭayarān (f) | تذكرة طيران |
| airline | ʃerket ṭayarān (f) | شركة طيران |
| airport | maṭār (m) | مطار |
| supersonic (adj) | χāreq lel ṣote | خارق للصوت |
| captain | kabten (m) | كابتن |
| crew | ṭa’m (m) | طقم |
| pilot | ṭayār (m) | طيّار |
| stewardess | moḍīfet ṭayarān (f) | مضيفة طيران |
| navigator | mallāḥ (m) | ملاّح |
| wings | agneḥa (pl) | أجنحة |
| tail | deyl (m) | ذيل |
| cockpit | kabīna (f) | كابينة |
| engine | motore (m) | موتور |
| undercarriage (landing gear) | ‘agalāt el hobūṭ (pl) | عجلات الهبوط |
| turbine | torbīna (f) | توربينة |
| propeller | marwaḥa (f) | مروّحة |
| black box | mosaggel el ṭayarān (m) | مسجّل الطيران |
| yoke (control column) | moqawwed el ṭayāra (m) | مقوّد الطيّارة |
| fuel | woqūd (m) | وقود |
| safety card | beṭā’et el salāma (f) | بطاقة السلامة |
| oxygen mask | mask el oksyʒīn (m) | ماسك الاوكسيجين |
| uniform | zayī muwaḥḥad (m) | زيّ موحّد |
| lifejacket | sotret nagah (f) | سترة نجاة |
| parachute | baraʃot (m) | باراشوت |
| takeoff | eqlā‘ (m) | إقلاع |
| to take off (vi) | aqla‘et | أقلعت |
| runway | modarrag el ṭa’erāṭ (m) | مدرّج الطائرات |
| visibility | ro’ya (f) | رؤية |
| flight (act of flying) | ṭayarān (m) | طيران |
| altitude | ertefā‘ (m) | إرتفاع |
| air pocket | geyb hawā’y (m) | جيب هوائي |
| seat | meq‘ad (m) | مقعد |
| headphones | samma‘āt ra’siya (pl) | سمّاعات رأسية |
| folding tray (tray table) | ṣeniya qabela lel ṭayī (f) | صينية قابلة للطيّ |
| airplane window | ʃebbāk el ṭayāra (m) | شبّاك الطيّارة |
| aisle | mamarr (m) | ممرّ |

## 25. Train

| | | |
|---|---|---|
| train | qeṭār, ʾaṭṭr (m) | قطار |
| commuter train | qeṭār rokkāb (m) | قطار ركّاب |
| express train | qeṭār saree' (m) | قطار سريع |
| diesel locomotive | qāṭeret dīzel (f) | قاطرة ديزل |
| steam locomotive | qāṭera boxariya (f) | قاطرة بخاريّة |
| coach, carriage | 'araba (f) | عربة |
| buffet car | 'arabet el ṭa'ām (f) | عربة الطعام |
| rails | qoḍbān (pl) | قضبان |
| railway | sekka ḥadīdiya (f) | سكّة حديديّة |
| sleeper (track support) | 'āreḍa sekket ḥadīd (f) | عارضة سكّة الحديد |
| platform (railway ~) | raṣīf (m) | رصيف |
| platform (~ 1, 2, etc.) | xaṭṭ (m) | خطّ |
| semaphore | semafore (m) | سيمافور |
| station | maḥaṭṭa (f) | محطّة |
| train driver | sawwāʾ (m) | سوّاق |
| porter (of luggage) | ʃayāl (m) | شيّال |
| carriage attendant | masʾūl 'arabet el qeṭār (m) | مسؤول عربة القطار |
| passenger | rākeb (m) | راكب |
| ticket inspector | kamsary (m) | كمسري |
| corridor (in train) | mamarr (m) | ممرّ |
| emergency brake | farāmel el ṭawāreʾ (pl) | فرامل الطوارئ |
| compartment | ɣorfa (f) | غرفة |
| berth | serīr (m) | سرير |
| upper berth | serīr 'olwy (m) | سرير علوّي |
| lower berth | serīr sofly (m) | سرير سفلي |
| bed linen, bedding | aɣṭeyet el serīr (pl) | أغطيّة السرير |
| ticket | tazkara (f) | تذكرة |
| timetable | gadwal (m) | جدوّل |
| information display | lawḥet ma'lomāt (f) | لوحة معلومات |
| to leave, to depart | ɣādar | غادر |
| departure (of a train) | moɣadra (f) | مغادرة |
| to arrive (ab. train) | weṣel | وصل |
| arrival | woṣūl (m) | وصول |
| to arrive by train | weṣel bel qeṭār | وصل بالقطار |
| to get on the train | rekeb el qeṭār | ركب القطار |
| to get off the train | nezel men el qeṭār | نزل من القطار |
| train crash | ḥeṭām qeṭār (m) | حطام قطار |
| to derail (vi) | xarag 'an xaṭṭ sīru | خرج عن خطّ سيره |
| steam locomotive | qāṭera boxariya (f) | قاطرة بخاريّة |
| stoker, fireman | 'aṭʃagy (m) | عطشجي |
| firebox | forn el moḥarrek (m) | فرن المحرّك |
| coal | faḥm (m) | فحم |

## 26. Ship

| | | |
|---|---|---|
| ship | safīna (f) | سفينة |
| vessel | safīna (f) | سفينة |
| steamship | baχera (f) | باخرة |
| riverboat | baχera nahriya (f) | باخرة نهرية |
| cruise ship | safīna seyaḥiya (f) | سفينة سياحيّة |
| cruiser | ṭarrād safīna baḥariya (m) | طرّاد سفينة بحريّة |
| yacht | yaχt (m) | يخت |
| tugboat | qāṭera baḥariya (f) | قاطرة بحريّة |
| barge | ṣandal (m) | صندل |
| ferry | ʿabbāra (f) | عبّارة |
| sailing ship | safīna ʃeraʿiya (m) | سفينة شراعيّة |
| brigantine | markeb ʃerāʿy (m) | مركب شراعي |
| ice breaker | moḥaṭṭemet galīd (f) | محطّمة جليد |
| submarine | ɣawwāṣa (f) | غوّاصة |
| boat (flat-bottomed ~) | markeb (m) | مركب |
| dinghy (lifeboat) | zawraʾ (m) | زورق |
| lifeboat | qāreb nagah (m) | قارب نجاة |
| motorboat | lunʃ (m) | لنش |
| captain | ʾobṭān (m) | قبطان |
| seaman | baḥḥār (m) | بحّار |
| sailor | baḥḥār (m) | بحّار |
| crew | ṭāqem (m) | طاقم |
| boatswain | rabbān (m) | ربّان |
| ship's boy | ṣaby el safīna (m) | صبي السفينة |
| cook | ṭabbāχ (m) | طبّاخ |
| ship's doctor | ṭabīb el safīna (m) | طبيب السفينة |
| deck | saṭ-ḥ el safīna (m) | سطح السفينة |
| mast | sāreya (f) | سارية |
| sail | ʃerāʿ (m) | شراع |
| hold | ʿanbar (m) | عنبر |
| bow (prow) | moʾaddema (m) | مقدّمة |
| stern | moʾaχeret el safīna (f) | مؤخّرة السفينة |
| oar | megdāf (m) | مجداف |
| screw propeller | marwaḥa (f) | مروّحة |
| cabin | kabīna (f) | كابينة |
| wardroom | ɣorfet el ṭaʿām wel rāḥa (f) | غرفة الطعام والراحة |
| engine room | qesm el ʾālāt (m) | قسم الآلات |
| bridge | borg el qeyāda (m) | برج القيادة |
| radio room | ɣorfet el lāselky (f) | غرفة اللاسلكي |
| wave (radio) | mouga (f) | موجة |
| logbook | segel el safīna (m) | سجل السفينة |
| spyglass | monzār (m) | منظار |
| bell | garas (m) | جرس |

| | | |
|---|---|---|
| flag | ʿalam (m) | علم |
| hawser (mooring ~) | ḥabl (m) | حبل |
| knot (bowline, etc.) | ʿoʾda (f) | عقدة |
| deckrails | drabzīn saṭ-ḥ el safīna (m) | درابزين سطح السفينة |
| gangway | sellem (m) | سلّم |
| anchor | marsāh (f) | مرساة |
| to weigh anchor | rafaʿ morsah | رفع مرساة |
| to drop anchor | rasa | رسا |
| anchor chain | selselet morsah (f) | سلسلة مرساة |
| port (harbour) | mināʾ (m) | ميناء |
| quay, wharf | marsa (m) | مرسى |
| to berth (moor) | rasa | رسا |
| to cast off | aqlaʿ | أقلع |
| trip, voyage | reḥla (f) | رحلة |
| cruise (sea trip) | reḥla baḥariya (f) | رحلة بحريّة |
| course (route) | masār (m) | مسار |
| route (itinerary) | ṭarīʾ (m) | طريق |
| fairway (safe water channel) | magra melāḥy (m) | مجرى ملاحيّ |
| shallows | meyāh ḍaḥla (f) | مياه ضحلة |
| to run aground | ganaḥ | جنح |
| storm | ʿāṣefa (f) | عاصفة |
| signal | eʃara (f) | إشارة |
| to sink (vi) | ɣereʾ | غرق |
| Man overboard! | saʾaṭ rāgil min el sefīna! | سقط راجل من السفينة! |
| SOS (distress signal) | nedāʾ eɣāsa (m) | نداء إغاثة |
| ring buoy | ṭoʾe nagah (m) | طوق نجاة |

# CITY

## 27. Urban transport

| | | |
|---|---|---|
| bus, coach | buṣ (m) | باص |
| tram | trām (m) | ترام |
| trolleybus | trolly buṣ (m) | ترولي باص |
| route (bus ~) | χaṭṭ (m) | خط |
| number (e.g. bus ~) | raqam (m) | رقم |
| to go by … | rāḥ be … | راح بـ ... |
| to get on (~ the bus) | rekeb | ركب |
| to get off … | nezel men | نزل من |
| stop (e.g. bus ~) | maw'af (m) | موّقف |
| next stop | el maḥaṭṭa el gaya (f) | المحطة الجايّة |
| terminus | 'āχer maw'af (m) | آخر موقف |
| timetable | gadwal (m) | جدوَل |
| to wait (vt) | estanna | إستنّى |
| ticket | tazkara (f) | تذكرة |
| fare | ogra (f) | أجرة |
| cashier (ticket seller) | kaʃier (m) | كاشيير |
| ticket inspection | taftīʃ el tazāker (m) | تفتيش التذاكر |
| ticket inspector | mofatteʃ tazāker (m) | مفتّش تذاكر |
| to be late (for …) | met'akχer | متأخّر |
| to miss (~ the train, etc.) | ta'akχar | تأخّر |
| to be in a hurry | mesta'gel | مستعجل |
| taxi, cab | taksi (m) | تاكسي |
| taxi driver | sawwā' taksi (m) | سوّاق تاكسي |
| by taxi | bel taksi | بالتاكسي |
| taxi rank | maw'ef taksi (m) | موّقف تاكسي |
| to call a taxi | kallem taksi | كلّم تاكسي |
| to take a taxi | aχad taksi | أخد تاكسي |
| traffic | ḥaraket el morūr (f) | حركة المرور |
| traffic jam | zaḥmet el morūr (f) | زحمة المرور |
| rush hour | sā'et el zorwa (f) | ساعة الذروة |
| to park (vi) | rakan | ركن |
| to park (vt) | rakan | ركن |
| car park | maw'ef el 'arabeyāt (m) | موقف العربيات |
| underground, tube | metro (m) | مترو |
| station | maḥaṭṭa (f) | محطّة |
| to take the tube | aχad el metro | أخد المترو |
| train | qeṭār, 'aṭṭr (m) | قطار |
| train station | maḥaṭṭet qeṭār (f) | محطّة قطار |

## 28. City. Life in the city

| | | |
|---|---|---|
| city, town | madīna (f) | مدينة |
| capital city | ʿāṣema (f) | عاصمة |
| village | qarya (f) | قرية |
| city map | xarīṭet el madinah (f) | خريطة المدينة |
| city centre | wesṭ el balad (m) | وسط البلد |
| suburb | ḍāḥeya (f) | ضاحية |
| suburban (adj) | el ḍawāḥy | الضواحي |
| outskirts | aṭrāf el madīna (pl) | أطراف المدينة |
| environs (suburbs) | ḍawāḥy el madīna (pl) | ضواحي المدينة |
| city block | ḥayī (m) | حي |
| residential block (area) | ḥayī sakany (m) | حي سكني |
| traffic | ḥaraket el morūr (f) | حركة المرور |
| traffic lights | eʃārāt el morūr (pl) | إشارات المرور |
| public transport | wasāʾel el naʾl (pl) | وسائل النقل |
| crossroads | taqāṭoʿ (m) | تقاطع |
| zebra crossing | maʿbar (m) | معبر |
| pedestrian subway | nafaʾ moʃāh (m) | نفق مشاه |
| to cross (~ the street) | ʿabar | عبر |
| pedestrian | māʃy (m) | ماشي |
| pavement | raṣīf (m) | رصيف |
| bridge | kobry (m) | كبري |
| embankment (river walk) | korneyʃ (m) | كورنيش |
| fountain | nafūra (f) | نافورة |
| allée (garden walkway) | mamʃa (m) | ممشى |
| park | ḥadīqa (f) | حديقة |
| boulevard | bolvār (m) | بولفار |
| square | medān (m) | ميدان |
| avenue (wide street) | ʃāreʿ (m) | شارع |
| street | ʃāreʿ (m) | شارع |
| side street | zoʾāʾ (m) | زقاق |
| dead end | ṭarīʾ masdūd (m) | طريق مسدود |
| house | beyt (m) | بيت |
| building | mabna (m) | مبنى |
| skyscraper | nāṭeḥet sahāb (f) | ناطحة سحاب |
| facade | waɣa (f) | واجهة |
| roof | saʾf (m) | سقف |
| window | ʃebbāk (m) | شبّاك |
| arch | qose (m) | قوس |
| column | ʿamūd (m) | عمود |
| corner | zawya (f) | زاوية |
| shop window | vatrīna (f) | فترينة |
| signboard (store sign, etc.) | yafṭa, lāfeta (f) | لافتة, يافطة |
| poster (e.g., playbill) | boster (m) | بوستر |
| advertising poster | boster eʿlān (m) | بوستر إعلان |

| | | |
|---|---|---|
| hoarding | lawḥet e'lanāt (f) | لوحة إعلانات |
| rubbish | zebāla (f) | زبالة |
| rubbish bin | ṣandū' zebāla (m) | صندوق زبالة |
| to litter (vi) | rama zebāla | رمى زبالة |
| rubbish dump | mazbala (f) | مزبلة |
| | | |
| telephone box | koʃk telefōn (m) | كشك تليفون |
| lamppost | 'amūd nūr (m) | عمود نور |
| bench (park ~) | korsy (m) | كرسي |
| | | |
| police officer | ʃorṭy (m) | شرطي |
| police | ʃorṭa (f) | شرطة |
| beggar | ʃaḥḥāt (m) | شحّات |
| homeless (n) | motaʃarred (m) | متشرّد |

## 29. Urban institutions

| | | |
|---|---|---|
| shop | maḥal (m) | محل |
| chemist, pharmacy | ṣaydaliya (f) | صيدليّة |
| optician (spectacles shop) | maḥal naḍḍārāt (m) | محل نضّارات |
| shopping centre | mole (m) | مول |
| supermarket | subermarket (m) | سوبرماركت |
| | | |
| bakery | maχbaz (m) | مخبز |
| baker | χabbāz (m) | خبّاز |
| cake shop | ḥalawāny (m) | حلواني |
| grocery shop | ba''āla (f) | بقّالة |
| butcher shop | gezāra (f) | جزارة |
| | | |
| greengrocer | dokkān χoḍār (m) | دكّان خضار |
| market | sū' (f) | سوق |
| | | |
| coffee bar | 'ahwa (f), kaféih (m) | قهوة, كافيه |
| restaurant | maṭ'am (m) | مطعم |
| pub, bar | bār (m) | بار |
| pizzeria | maḥal pizza (m) | محل بيتزا |
| | | |
| hairdresser | ṣalone ḥelā'a (m) | صالون حلاقة |
| post office | maktab el barīd (m) | مكتب البريد |
| dry cleaners | dray klīn (m) | دراي كلين |
| photo studio | estudio taṣwīr (m) | إستوديو تصوير |
| | | |
| shoe shop | maḥal gezam (m) | محل جزم |
| bookshop | maḥal kotob (m) | محل كتب |
| sports shop | maḥal mostalzamāt reyaḍiya (m) | محل مستلزمات رياضية |
| | | |
| clothes repair shop | maḥal χeyāṭet malābes (m) | محل خياطة ملابس |
| formal wear hire | ta'gīr malābes rasmiya (m) | تأجير ملابس رسمية |
| video rental shop | maḥal ta'gīr video (m) | محل تأجير فيديو |
| | | |
| circus | serk (m) | سيرك |
| zoo | ḥadīqet el ḥayawān (f) | حديقة حيوان |
| cinema | sinema (f) | سينما |

| | | |
|---|---|---|
| museum | mat-ḥaf (m) | متحف |
| library | maktaba (f) | مكتبة |
| theatre | masraḥ (m) | مسرح |
| opera (opera house) | obra (f) | أوبرا |
| nightclub | malha leyly (m) | ملهى ليّلي |
| casino | kazino (m) | كازينو |
| mosque | masged (m) | مسجد |
| synagogue | kenīs (m) | كنيس |
| cathedral | katedra'iya (f) | كاتدرائية |
| temple | ma'bad (m) | معبد |
| church | kenīsa (f) | كنيسة |
| college | kolliya (m) | كليّة |
| university | gam'a (f) | جامعة |
| school | madrasa (f) | مدرسة |
| prefecture | moqaṭ'a (f) | مقاطعة |
| town hall | baladiya (f) | بلديّة |
| hotel | fondo' (m) | فندق |
| bank | bank (m) | بنك |
| embassy | safāra (f) | سفارة |
| travel agency | ʃerket seyāḥa (f) | شركة سياحة |
| information office | maktab el este'lāmāt (m) | مكتب الإستعلامات |
| currency exchange | ṣarrāfa (f) | صرّافة |
| underground, tube | metro (m) | مترو |
| hospital | mostaʃfa (m) | مستشفى |
| petrol station | maḥaṭṭet banzīn (f) | محطّة بنزين |
| car park | maw'ef el 'arabeyāt (m) | موقف العربيات |

## 30. Signs

| | | |
|---|---|---|
| signboard (store sign, etc.) | yafṭa, lāfeta (f) | لافتة, يافطة |
| notice (door sign, etc.) | bayān (m) | بيان |
| poster | boster (m) | بوستر |
| direction sign | 'alāmet (f) | علامة إتجاه |
| arrow (sign) | 'alāmet eʃāra (f) | علامة إشارة |
| caution | taḥzīr (m) | تحذير |
| warning sign | lāfetat taḥzīr (f) | لافتة تحذير |
| to warn (vt) | ḥazzar | حذّر |
| rest day (weekly ~) | yome 'oṭla (m) | يوم عطلة |
| timetable (schedule) | gadwal (m) | جدوَل |
| opening hours | aw'āt el 'amal (pl) | أوقات العمل |
| WELCOME! | ahlan w sahlan! | أهلاً وسهلا! |
| ENTRANCE | doχūl | دخول |
| WAY OUT | χorūg | خروج |
| PUSH | edfa' | إدفع |

| | | |
|---|---|---|
| PULL | es-ḥab | إسحب |
| OPEN | maftūḥ | مفتوح |
| CLOSED | moɣlaq | مغلق |
| | | |
| WOMEN | lel sayedāt | للسيدات |
| MEN | lel regāl | للرجال |
| | | |
| DISCOUNTS | χoṣomāt | خصومات |
| SALE | taχfeḍāt | تخفيضات |
| NEW! | gedīd! | جديد! |
| FREE | maggānan | مجّاناً |
| | | |
| ATTENTION! | entebāh! | إنتباه! |
| NO VACANCIES | koll el amāken maḥgūza | كلّ الأماكن محجوزة |
| RESERVED | maḥgūz | محجوز |
| | | |
| ADMINISTRATION | edāra | إدارة |
| STAFF ONLY | lel ʿamelīn faqaṭ | للعاملين فقط |
| | | |
| BEWARE OF THE DOG! | eḥzar wogūd kalb | إحذر وجود الكلب |
| NO SMOKING | mamnūʿ el tadχīn | ممنوع التدخين |
| DO NOT TOUCH! | ʿadam el lams | عدم اللمس |
| | | |
| DANGEROUS | χaṭīr | خطير |
| DANGER | χaṭar | خطر |
| HIGH VOLTAGE | tayār ʿāly | تيّار عالي |
| NO SWIMMING! | el sebāḥa mamnūʿa | السباحة ممنوعة |
| OUT OF ORDER | moʿaṭṭal | معطّل |
| | | |
| FLAMMABLE | sareeʿ el eʃteʿāl | سريع الإشتعال |
| FORBIDDEN | mamnūʿ | ممنوع |
| NO TRESPASSING! | mamnūʿ el morūr | ممنوع المرور |
| WET PAINT | eḥzar ṭelāʾ ɣayr gāf | احذر طلاء غير جاف |

## 31. Shopping

| | | |
|---|---|---|
| to buy (purchase) | eʃtara | إشترى |
| shopping | ḥāga (f) | حاجة |
| to go shopping | eʃtara | إشترى |
| shopping | ʃobbing (m) | شوبينج |
| | | |
| to be open (ab. shop) | maftūḥ | مفتوح |
| to be closed | moɣlaq | مغلق |
| | | |
| footwear, shoes | gezam (pl) | جزم |
| clothes, clothing | malābes (pl) | ملابس |
| cosmetics | mawād tagmīl (pl) | مواد تجميل |
| food products | akl (m) | أكل |
| gift, present | hediya (f) | هديّة |
| | | |
| shop assistant (masc.) | bayāʿ (m) | بيّاع |
| shop assistant (fem.) | bayāʿa (f) | بيّاعة |
| cash desk | ṣandūʾ el dafʿ (m) | صندوق الدفع |
| mirror | merāya (f) | مراية |

| | | |
|---|---|---|
| counter (shop ~) | manḍada (f) | منضدة |
| fitting room | ɣorfet el 'eyās (f) | غرفة القياس |
| to try on | garrab | جرّب |
| to fit (ab. dress, etc.) | nāseb | ناسب |
| to fancy (vt) | 'agab | عجب |
| price | se'r (m) | سعر |
| price tag | tiket el se'r (m) | تيكت السعر |
| to cost (vt) | kallef | كلّف |
| How much? | bekām? | بكام؟ |
| discount | χaṣm (m) | خصم |
| inexpensive (adj) | meʃ ɣāly | مش غالي |
| cheap (adj) | reχīṣ | رخيص |
| expensive (adj) | ɣāly | غالي |
| It's expensive | da ɣāly | ده غالي |
| hire (n) | este'gār (m) | إستئجار |
| to hire (~ a dinner jacket) | est'gar | إستأجر |
| credit (trade credit) | e'temān (m) | إئتمان |
| on credit (adv) | bel ta'seeṭ | بالتقسيط |

# CLOTHING & ACCESSORIES

## 32. Outerwear. Coats

| | | |
|---|---|---|
| clothes | malābes (pl) | ملابس |
| outerwear | malābes fo'aniya (pl) | ملابس فوقانيّة |
| winter clothing | malābes ʃetwiya (pl) | ملابس شتويّة |
| coat (overcoat) | balṭo (m) | بالطو |
| fur coat | balṭo farww (m) | بالطو فروّ |
| fur jacket | ʒaket farww (m) | جاكيت فروّ |
| down coat | balṭo maḥʃy rīʃ (m) | بالطو محشي ريش |
| jacket (e.g. leather ~) | ʒæket (m) | جاكيت |
| raincoat (trenchcoat, etc.) | ʒæket lel maṭar (m) | جاكيت للمطر |
| waterproof (adj) | wāqy men el maya | واقي من الميّة |

## 33. Men's & women's clothing

| | | |
|---|---|---|
| shirt (button shirt) | 'amīṣ (m) | قميص |
| trousers | banṭalone (f) | بنطلون |
| jeans | ʒeans (m) | جينز |
| suit jacket | ʒæket (f) | جاكت |
| suit | badla (f) | بدلة |
| dress (frock) | fostān (m) | فستان |
| skirt | ʒība (f) | جيبة |
| blouse | bloza (f) | بلوزة |
| knitted jacket (cardigan, etc.) | kardigan (m) | كارديجن |
| jacket (of a woman's suit) | ʒæket (m) | جاكيت |
| T-shirt | ti ʃirt (m) | تي شيرت |
| shorts (short trousers) | ʃort (m) | شورت |
| tracksuit | treneng (m) | ترينج |
| bathrobe | robe el ḥammām (m) | روب حمّام |
| pyjamas | beʒāma (f) | بيجاما |
| jumper (sweater) | blover (f) | بلوفر |
| pullover | blover (m) | بلوفر |
| waistcoat | vest (m) | فيست |
| tailcoat | badlet sahra ṭawīla (f) | بدلة سهرة طويلة |
| dinner suit | badla (f) | بدلة |
| uniform | zayī muwaḥḥad (m) | زيّ موحّد |
| workwear | lebs el ʃoɣl (m) | لبس الشغل |
| boiler suit | overall (m) | اوفر اول |
| coat (e.g. doctor's smock) | balṭo (m) | بالطو |

## 34. Clothing. Underwear

| | | |
|---|---|---|
| underwear | malābes dāxeliya (pl) | ملابس داخلية |
| pants | sirwāl dāxly rigāly (m) | سروال داخلي رجاليّ |
| panties | sirwāl dāxly nisā'y (m) | سروال داخلي نسائيّ |
| vest (singlet) | fanella (f) | فانلّا |
| socks | ʃarāb (m) | شراب |
| nightdress | 'amīṣ nome (m) | قميص نوم |
| bra | setyāna (f) | ستيانة |
| knee highs (knee-high socks) | ʃarabāt ṭawīla (pl) | شرابات طويلة |
| tights | klone (m) | كلون |
| stockings (hold ups) | gawāreb (pl) | جوارب |
| swimsuit, bikini | mayo (m) | مايّوه |

## 35. Headwear

| | | |
|---|---|---|
| hat | ṭa'iya (f) | طاقيّة |
| trilby hat | borneyṭa (f) | برنيطة |
| baseball cap | base bāl kāb (m) | بيس بول كاب |
| flatcap | ṭa'iya mosaṭṭaḥa (f) | طاقيّة مسطحة |
| beret | bereyh (m) | بيريه |
| hood | ɣaṭa' (f) | غطاء |
| panama hat | qobba'et banama (f) | قبّعة بناما |
| knit cap (knitted hat) | ays kāb (m) | آيس كاب |
| headscarf | eʃarb (m) | إيشارب |
| women's hat | borneyṭa (f) | برنيطة |
| hard hat | xawza (f) | خوذة |
| forage cap | kāb (m) | كاب |
| helmet | xawza (f) | خوذة |
| bowler | qobba'a (f) | قبّعة |
| top hat | qobba'a rasmiya (f) | قبّعة رسمية |

## 36. Footwear

| | | |
|---|---|---|
| footwear | gezam (pl) | جزم |
| shoes (men's shoes) | gazma (f) | جزمة |
| shoes (women's shoes) | gazma (f) | جزمة |
| boots (e.g., cowboy ~) | būt (m) | بوت |
| carpet slippers | ʃebʃeb (m) | شبشب |
| trainers | kotʃy tennis (m) | كوتشي تنس |
| trainers | kotʃy (m) | كوتشي |
| sandals | ṣandal (pl) | صندل |
| cobbler (shoe repairer) | eskāfy (m) | إسكافي |
| heel | ka'b (m) | كعب |

| | | |
|---|---|---|
| pair (of shoes) | goze (m) | جوز |
| lace (shoelace) | ʃerīṭ (m) | شريط |
| to lace up (vt) | rabaṭ | ربط |
| shoehorn | labbāsa el gazma (f) | لبّاسة الجزمة |
| shoe polish | warnīʃ el gazma (m) | ورنيش الجزمة |

## 37. Personal accessories

| | | |
|---|---|---|
| gloves | gwanty (m) | جوانتي |
| mittens | gwanty men ɣeyr aṣābeʿ (m) | جوانتي من غير أصابع |
| scarf (muffler) | skarf (m) | سكارف |
| glasses | naḍḍāra (f) | نظّارة |
| frame (eyeglass ~) | eṭār (m) | إطار |
| umbrella | ʃamsiya (f) | شمسيّة |
| walking stick | ʿaṣāya (f) | عصاية |
| hairbrush | forʃet ʃaʿr (f) | فرشة شعر |
| fan | marwaḥa (f) | مروّحة |
| tie (necktie) | karavetta (f) | كرافتة |
| bow tie | bebyona (m) | بيبيونة |
| braces | ḥammala (f) | حمّالة |
| handkerchief | mandīl (m) | منديل |
| comb | meʃṭ (m) | مشط |
| hair slide | dabbūs (m) | دبّوس |
| hairpin | bensa (m) | بنسة |
| buckle | bokla (f) | بكلة |
| belt | ḥezām (m) | حزام |
| shoulder strap | ḥammalet el ketf (f) | حمّالة الكتف |
| bag (handbag) | ʃanṭa (f) | شنطة |
| handbag | ʃanṭet yad (f) | شنطة يد |
| rucksack | ʃanṭet ḍahr (f) | شنطة ظهر |

## 38. Clothing. Miscellaneous

| | | |
|---|---|---|
| fashion | mūḍa (f) | موضة |
| in vogue (adj) | fel moḍa | في الموضة |
| fashion designer | moṣammem azyāʾ (m) | مصمّم أزياء |
| collar | yāʾa (f) | ياقة |
| pocket | geyb (m) | جيب |
| pocket (as adj) | geyb | جيب |
| sleeve | komm (m) | كمّ |
| hanging loop | ʿelāqa (f) | علّاقة |
| flies (on trousers) | lesān (m) | لسان |
| zip (fastener) | sosta (f) | سوستة |
| fastener | maʃbak (m) | مشبك |
| button | zerr (m) | زرّ |

| | | |
|---|---|---|
| buttonhole | ʿarwa (f) | عروة |
| to come off (ab. button) | weʾeʿ | وقع |
| | | |
| to sew (vi, vt) | χayaṭ | خيّط |
| to embroider (vi, vt) | ṭarraz | طرّز |
| embroidery | taṭrīz (m) | تطريز |
| sewing needle | ebra (f) | إبرة |
| thread | χeyṭ (m) | خيط |
| seam | derz (m) | درز |
| | | |
| to get dirty (vi) | ettwassaχ | إتّوسّخ |
| stain (mark, spot) | boʾʿa (f) | بقعة |
| to crease, to crumple | takarmaʃ | تكرمش |
| to tear, to rip (vt) | ʾaṭaʿ | قطع |
| clothes moth | ʿetta (f) | عثّة |

## 39. Personal care. Cosmetics

| | | |
|---|---|---|
| toothpaste | maʿgūn asnān (m) | معجون أسنان |
| toothbrush | forʃet senān (f) | فرشة أسنان |
| to clean one's teeth | naḍḍaf el asnān | نظّف الأسنان |
| | | |
| razor | mūs (m) | موس |
| shaving cream | krīm ḥelāʾa (m) | كريم حلاقة |
| to shave (vi) | ḥalaʾ | حلق |
| | | |
| soap | ṣabūn (m) | صابون |
| shampoo | ʃambū (m) | شامبو |
| | | |
| scissors | maʾaṣ (m) | مقص |
| nail file | mabrad (m) | مبرد |
| nail clippers | melʾaṭ (m) | ملقط |
| tweezers | melʾaṭ (m) | ملقط |
| | | |
| cosmetics | mawād tagmīl (pl) | مواد تجميل |
| face mask | mask (m) | ماسك |
| manicure | monekīr (m) | مونيكير |
| to have a manicure | ʿamal monikīr | عمل مونيكير |
| pedicure | badikīr (m) | باديكير |
| | | |
| make-up bag | ʃanṭet mekyāʒ (f) | شنطة مكياج |
| face powder | bodret weʃ (f) | بودرة وش |
| powder compact | ʿelbet bodra (f) | علبة بودرة |
| blusher | aḥmar χodūd (m) | أحمر خدود |
| | | |
| perfume (bottled) | barfān (m) | بارفان |
| toilet water (lotion) | kolonya (f) | كولونيا |
| lotion | loʃion (m) | لوشن |
| cologne | kolonya (f) | كولونيا |
| | | |
| eyeshadow | eyeʃadow (m) | اي شادو |
| eyeliner | koḥl (m) | كحل |
| mascara | maskara (f) | ماسكارا |
| lipstick | rūʒ (m) | روج |

| | | |
|---|---|---|
| nail polish | monekīr (m) | مونيكير |
| hair spray | mosabbet el ʃa'r (m) | مثبّت الشعر |
| deodorant | mozīl 'ara' (m) | مزيل عرق |
| cream | krīm (m) | كريم |
| face cream | krīm lel weʃ (m) | كريم للوش |
| hand cream | krīm eyd (m) | كريم أيد |
| anti-wrinkle cream | krīm moḍād lel tagaʿīd (m) | كريم مضاد للتجاعيد |
| day cream | krīm en nahār (m) | كريم النهار |
| night cream | krīm el leyl (m) | كريم الليل |
| day (as adj) | nahāry | نهاري |
| night (as adj) | layly | ليّلي |
| tampon | tambon (m) | تانبون |
| toilet paper (toilet roll) | wara' twalet (m) | ورق تواليت |
| hair dryer | seʃwār (m) | سشوار |

## 40. Watches. Clocks

| | | |
|---|---|---|
| watch (wristwatch) | sā'a (f) | ساعة |
| dial | wag-h el sā'a (m) | وجه الساعة |
| hand (clock, watch) | 'a'rab el sā'a (m) | عقرب الساعة |
| metal bracelet | ʃerīṭ sā'a ma'daniya (m) | شريط ساعة معدنية |
| watch strap | ʃerīṭ el sā'a (m) | شريط الساعة |
| battery | baṭṭariya (f) | بطّاريّة |
| to be flat (battery) | χelṣet | خلصت |
| to change a battery | ɣayar el baṭṭariya | غيّر البطّاريّة |
| to run fast | saba' | سبق |
| to run slow | ta'akχar | تأخّر |
| wall clock | sā'et ḥeyṭa (f) | ساعة حيطة |
| hourglass | sā'a ramliya (f) | ساعة رمليّة |
| sundial | sā'a ʃamsiya (f) | ساعة شمسيّة |
| alarm clock | monabbeh (m) | منبّه |
| watchmaker | sa'āty (m) | ساعاتي |
| to repair (vt) | ṣallaḥ | صلّح |

# EVERYDAY EXPERIENCE

## 41. Money

| | | |
|---|---|---|
| money | folūs (pl) | فلوس |
| currency exchange | taḥwīl ʿomla (m) | تحويل عملة |
| exchange rate | seʿr el ṣarf (m) | سعر الصرف |
| cashpoint | makinet ṣarrāf ʾāly (f) | ماكينة صرّاف آلي |
| coin | ʾerʃ (m) | قرش |
| dollar | dolār (m) | دولار |
| euro | yoro (m) | يورو |
| lira | lira (f) | ليرة |
| Deutschmark | el mark el almāny (m) | المارك الألماني |
| franc | frank (m) | فرنك |
| pound sterling | geneyh esterlīny (m) | جنيه استرليني |
| yen | yen (m) | ين |
| debt | deyn (m) | دين |
| debtor | modīn (m) | مدين |
| to lend (money) | sallef | سلّف |
| to borrow (vi, vt) | estalaf | إستلف |
| bank | bank (m) | بنك |
| account | ḥesāb (m) | حساب |
| to deposit (vt) | awdaʿ | أودع |
| to deposit into the account | awdaʿ fel ḥesāb | أودّع في الحساب |
| to withdraw (vt) | saḥab men el ḥesāb | سحب من الحساب |
| credit card | kredit kard (f) | كريدت كارد |
| cash | kæʃ (m) | كاش |
| cheque | ʃīk (m) | شيك |
| to write a cheque | katab ʃīk | كتب شيك |
| chequebook | daftar ʃikāt (m) | دفتر شيكات |
| wallet | maḥfaẓa (f) | محفظة |
| purse | maḥfazet fakka (f) | محفظة فكّة |
| safe | χazzāna (f) | خزّانة |
| heir | wāres (m) | وارث |
| inheritance | werāsa (f) | وراثة |
| fortune (wealth) | sarwa (f) | ثروّة |
| lease | ʿaʾd el egār (m) | عقد الإيجار |
| rent (money) | ogret el sakan (f) | أجرة السكن |
| to rent (sth from sb) | estʾgar | إستأجر |
| price | seʿr (m) | سعر |
| cost | taman (m) | ثمن |

| | | |
|---|---|---|
| sum | mablaɣ (m) | مبلغ |
| to spend (vt) | ṣaraf | صرف |
| expenses | maṣarīf (pl) | مصاريف |
| to economize (vi, vt) | waffar | وفّر |
| economical | mowaffer | موّفر |
| to pay (vi, vt) | dafaʿ | دفع |
| payment | dafʿ (m) | دفع |
| change (give the ~) | el bā'y (m) | الباقي |
| tax | ḍarība (f) | ضريبة |
| fine | ɣarāma (f) | غرامة |
| to fine (vt) | faraḍ ɣarāma | فرض غرامة |

## 42. Post. Postal service

| | | |
|---|---|---|
| post office | maktab el barīd (m) | مكتب البريد |
| post (letters, etc.) | el barīd (m) | البريد |
| postman | sāʿy el barīd (m) | ساعي البريد |
| opening hours | aw'āt el ʿamal (pl) | أوقات العمل |
| letter | resāla (f) | رسالة |
| registered letter | resāla mosaggala (f) | رسالة مسجّلة |
| postcard | kart barīdy (m) | كرت بريدي |
| telegram | barqiya (f) | برقيّة |
| parcel | ṭard (m) | طرد |
| money transfer | ḥewāla māliya (f) | حوالة مالية |
| to receive (vt) | estalam | إستلم |
| to send (vt) | arsal | أرسل |
| sending | ersāl (m) | إرسال |
| address | ʿenwān (m) | عنوان |
| postcode | raqam el barīd (m) | رقم البريد |
| sender | morsel (m) | مرسل |
| receiver | morsel elayh (m) | مرسل إليه |
| name (first name) | esm (m) | اسم |
| surname (last name) | esm el ʿa'ela (m) | اسم العائلة |
| postage rate | taʿrīfa (f) | تعريفة |
| standard (adj) | ʿādy | عادي |
| economical (adj) | mowaffer | موّفر |
| weight | wazn (m) | وزن |
| to weigh (~ letters) | wazan | وزن |
| envelope | ẓarf (m) | ظرف |
| postage stamp | ṭābeʿ (m) | طابع |
| to stamp an envelope | alṣaq ṭābeʿ | ألصق طابع |

## 43. Banking

| | | |
|---|---|---|
| bank | bank (m) | بنك |
| branch (of a bank) | farʿ (m) | فرع |

| | | |
|---|---|---|
| consultant | mowazzaf bank (m) | موظّف بنك |
| manager (director) | modīr (m) | مدير |
| bank account | ḥesāb bank (m) | حساب بنك |
| account number | raqam el ḥesāb (m) | رقم الحساب |
| current account | ḥesāb gāry (m) | حساب جاري |
| deposit account | ḥesāb tawfīr (m) | حساب توّفير |
| to open an account | fataḥ ḥesāb | فتح حساب |
| to close the account | 'afal ḥesāb | قفل حساب |
| to deposit into the account | awda' fel ḥesāb | أودع في الحساب |
| to withdraw (vt) | saḥab men el ḥesāb | سحب من الحساب |
| deposit | wadee'a (f) | وديعة |
| to make a deposit | awda' | أودع |
| wire transfer | ḥewāla maṣrefiya (f) | حوالة مصرفيّة |
| to wire, to transfer | ḥawwel | حوّل |
| sum | mablaɣ (m) | مبلغ |
| How much? | kām? | كام؟ |
| signature | tawqee' (m) | توقيع |
| to sign (vt) | waqqa' | وقّع |
| credit card | kredit kard (f) | كريدت كارد |
| code (PIN code) | kōd (m) | كود |
| credit card number | raqam el kredit kard (m) | رقم الكريدت كارد |
| cashpoint | makinet ṣarrāf 'āly (f) | ماكينة صرّاف آلي |
| cheque | ʃīk (m) | شيك |
| to write a cheque | katab ʃīk | كتب شيك |
| chequebook | daftar ʃikāt (m) | دفتر شيكات |
| loan (bank ~) | qarḍ (m) | قرض |
| to apply for a loan | 'addem ṭalab 'ala qarḍ | قدّم طلب على قرض |
| to get a loan | ḥaṣal 'ala qarḍ | حصل على قرض |
| to give a loan | edda qarḍ | ادّى قرض |
| guarantee | ḍamān (m) | ضمان |

## 44. Telephone. Phone conversation

| | | |
|---|---|---|
| telephone | telefon (m) | تليفون |
| mobile phone | mobile (m) | موبايل |
| answerphone | gehāz radd 'alal mokalmāt (m) | جهاز ردّ على المكالمات |
| to call (by phone) | ettaṣal | إتّصل |
| call, ring | mokalma telefoniya (f) | مكالمة تليفونية |
| to dial a number | ettaṣal be raqam | إتّصل برقم |
| Hello! | alo! | ألو! |
| to ask (vt) | sa'al | سأل |
| to answer (vi, vt) | radd | ردّ |
| to hear (vt) | seme' | سمع |
| well (adv) | kewayes | كويّس |

| | | |
|---|---|---|
| not well (adv) | meʃ kowayīs | مش كويّس |
| noises (interference) | taʃwīʃ (m) | تشويش |
| receiver | sammāʿa (f) | سمّاعة |
| to pick up (~ the phone) | rafaʿ el sammāʿa | رفع السمّاعة |
| to hang up (~ the phone) | ʾafal el sammāʿa | قفل السمّاعة |
| busy (engaged) | maʃɣūl | مشغول |
| to ring (ab. phone) | rann | رن |
| telephone book | dalīl el telefone (m) | دليل التليفون |
| local (adj) | maḥalliya | ة محلّيّة |
| local call | mokalma maḥalliya (f) | مكالمة محلّيّة |
| trunk (e.g. ~ call) | biʿīd | بعيد |
| trunk call | mokalma biʿīda (f) | مكالمة بعيدة المدى |
| international (adj) | dowly | دوّلي |
| international call | mokalma dowliya (f) | مكالمة دوليّة |

## 45. Mobile telephone

| | | |
|---|---|---|
| mobile phone | mobile (m) | موبايل |
| display | ʿarḍ (m) | عرض |
| button | zerr (m) | زر |
| SIM card | sim kard (m) | سيم كارد |
| battery | baṭṭariya (f) | بطّاريّة |
| to be flat (battery) | χelṣet | خلصت |
| charger | ʃāḥen (m) | شاحن |
| menu | qāʾema (f) | قائمة |
| settings | awḍāʿ (pl) | أوضاع |
| tune (melody) | naɣama (f) | نغمة |
| to select (vt) | eχtār | إختار |
| calculator | ʾāla ḥasba (f) | آلة حاسبة |
| voice mail | barīd ṣawty (m) | بريد صوتي |
| alarm clock | monabbeh (m) | منبّه |
| contacts | gehāt el etteṣāl (pl) | جهات الإتّصال |
| SMS (text message) | resāla ʾaṣīra ɛsɛmɛs (f) | sms رسالة قصيرة |
| subscriber | moʃtarek (m) | مشترك |

## 46. Stationery

| | | |
|---|---|---|
| ballpoint pen | ʾalam gāf (m) | قلم جاف |
| fountain pen | ʾalam rīʃa (m) | قلم ريشة |
| pencil | ʾalam roṣāṣ (m) | قلم رصاص |
| highlighter | markar (m) | ماركر |
| felt-tip pen | ʾalam fulumaster (m) | قلم فلوماستر |
| notepad | mozakkera (f) | مذكّرة |
| diary | gadwal el aʿmāl (m) | جدول الأعمال |

| | | |
|---|---|---|
| ruler | masṭara (f) | مسطرة |
| calculator | 'āla ḥasba (f) | آلة حاسبة |
| rubber | astīka (f) | استيكة |
| drawing pin | dabbūs (m) | دبّوس |
| paper clip | dabbūs wara' (m) | دبّوس ورق |
| glue | ṣamɣ (m) | صمغ |
| stapler | dabbāsa (f) | دبّاسة |
| hole punch | χarrāma (m) | خرّامة |
| pencil sharpener | barrāya (f) | برّاية |

## 47. Foreign languages

| | | |
|---|---|---|
| language | loɣa (f) | لغة |
| foreign (adj) | agnaby | أجنبيّ |
| foreign language | loɣa agnabiya (f) | لغة أجنبية |
| to study (vt) | daras | درس |
| to learn (language, etc.) | ta'allam | تعلّم |
| to read (vi, vt) | 'ara | قرأ |
| to speak (vi, vt) | kallem | كلّم |
| to understand (vt) | fehem | فهم |
| to write (vt) | katab | كتب |
| fast (adv) | bosor'a | بسرعة |
| slowly (adv) | bo boṭ' | ببطء |
| fluently (adv) | beṭalāqa | بطلاقة |
| rules | qawā'ed (pl) | قواعد |
| grammar | el naḥw wel ṣarf (m) | النحو والصرف |
| vocabulary | mofradāt el loɣa (pl) | مفردات اللغة |
| phonetics | ṣawtīāt (pl) | صوتيات |
| textbook | ketāb ta'līm (m) | كتاب تعليم |
| dictionary | qamūs (m) | قاموس |
| teach-yourself book | ketāb ta'līm zāty (m) | كتاب تعليم ذاتي |
| phrasebook | ketāb lel 'ebarāt el ʃā'e'a (m) | كتاب للعبارت الشائعة |
| cassette, tape | kasett (m) | كاسيت |
| videotape | ʃerīṭ video (m) | شريط فيديو |
| CD, compact disc | sidī (m) | سي دي |
| DVD | dividī (m) | دي في دي |
| alphabet | abgadiya (f) | أبجدية |
| to spell (vt) | tahagga | تهجّى |
| pronunciation | noṭ' (m) | نطق |
| accent | lahga (f) | لهجة |
| with an accent | be lahga | بـ لهجة |
| without an accent | men ɣeyr lahga | من غير لهجة |
| word | kelma (f) | كلمة |
| meaning | ma'na (m) | معنى |
| course (e.g. a French ~) | dawra (f) | دورة |

| | | |
|---|---|---|
| to sign up | saggel esmo | سجّل إسمه |
| teacher | modarres (m) | مدرّس |
| translation (process) | targama (f) | ترجمة |
| translation (text, etc.) | targama (f) | ترجمة |
| translator | motargem (m) | مترجم |
| interpreter | motargem fawwry (m) | مترجم فوّري |
| polyglot | ʻalīm beʻeddet loɣāt (m) | عليم بعدّة لغات |
| memory | zākera (f) | ذاكرة |

# MEALS. RESTAURANT

## 48. Table setting

| | | |
|---|---|---|
| spoon | maʿlaʾa (f) | معلقة |
| knife | sekkīna (f) | سكّينة |
| fork | ʃawka (f) | شوكة |
| cup (e.g., coffee ~) | fengān (m) | فنجان |
| plate (dinner ~) | ṭabaʾ (m) | طبق |
| saucer | ṭabaʾ fengān (m) | طبق فنجان |
| serviette | mandīl waraʾ (m) | منديل ورق |
| toothpick | χallet senān (f) | خلة سنان |

## 49. Restaurant

| | | |
|---|---|---|
| restaurant | maṭʿam (m) | مطعم |
| coffee bar | ʾahwa (f), kaféih (m) | قهوة, كافيه |
| pub, bar | bār (m) | بار |
| tearoom | ṣalone ʃāy (m) | صالون شاي |
| waiter | garsone (m) | جرسون |
| waitress | garsona (f) | جرسونة |
| barman | bārman (m) | بارمان |
| menu | qāʾemet el ṭaʿām (f) | قائمة طعام |
| wine list | qāʾemet el χomūr (f) | قائمة خمور |
| to book a table | ḥagaz sofra | حجز سفرة |
| course, dish | wagba (f) | وجبة |
| to order (meal) | ṭalab | طلب |
| to make an order | ṭalab | طلب |
| aperitif | ʃarāb (m) | شراب |
| starter | moqabbelāt (pl) | مقبّلات |
| dessert, pudding | ḥalawīāt (pl) | حلويّات |
| bill | ḥesāb (m) | حساب |
| to pay the bill | dafaʿ el ḥesāb | دفع الحساب |
| to give change | edda el bāʾy | ادّي الباقي |
| tip | baʾʃīʃ (m) | بقشيش |

## 50. Meals

| | | |
|---|---|---|
| food | akl (m) | أكل |
| to eat (vi, vt) | akal | أكل |

| | | |
|---|---|---|
| breakfast | foṭūr (m) | فطور |
| to have breakfast | feṭer | فطر |
| lunch | ɣada' (m) | غداء |
| to have lunch | etɣadda | إتغدّى |
| dinner | 'aʃā' (m) | عشاء |
| to have dinner | et'asʃa | إتعشّى |
| | | |
| appetite | ʃahiya (f) | شهيّة |
| Enjoy your meal! | bel hana wel ʃefa! | !بالهنا والشفا |
| | | |
| to open (~ a bottle) | fataḥ | فتح |
| to spill (liquid) | dala' | دلق |
| to spill out (vi) | dala' | دلق |
| | | |
| to boil (vi) | ɣely | غلى |
| to boil (vt) | ɣely | غلى |
| boiled (~ water) | maɣly | مغلي |
| to chill, cool down (vt) | barrad | برّد |
| to chill (vi) | barrad | برّد |
| | | |
| taste, flavour | ṭa'm (m) | طعم |
| aftertaste | ṭa'm ma ba'd el mazāq (m) | طعم ما بعد المذاق |
| | | |
| to slim down (lose weight) | χass | خسّ |
| diet | reʒīm (m) | رجيم |
| vitamin | vitamīn (m) | فيتامين |
| calorie | so'ra ḥarāriya (f) | سعرة حراريّة |
| vegetarian (n) | nabāty (m) | نباتي |
| vegetarian (adj) | nabāty | نباتي |
| | | |
| fats (nutrient) | dohūn (pl) | دهون |
| proteins | brotenāt (pl) | بروتينات |
| carbohydrates | naʃawīāt (pl) | نشويّات |
| slice (of lemon, ham) | ʃarīḥa (f) | شريحة |
| piece (of cake, pie) | 'eṭ'a (f) | قطعة |
| crumb (of bread, cake, etc.) | fattāta (f) | فتاتة |

## 51. Cooked dishes

| | | |
|---|---|---|
| course, dish | wagba (f) | وجبة |
| cuisine | maṭbaχ (m) | مطبخ |
| recipe | waṣfa (f) | وصفة |
| portion | naṣīb (m) | نصيب |
| | | |
| salad | solṭa (f) | سلطة |
| soup | ʃorba (f) | شوربة |
| | | |
| clear soup (broth) | mara'a (m) | مرقة |
| sandwich (bread) | sandawitʃ (m) | ساندويتش |
| fried eggs | beyḍ ma'ly (m) | بيض مقلي |
| | | |
| hamburger (beefburger) | hamburger (m) | هامبورجر |
| beefsteak | steak laḥm (m) | ستيك لحم |
| side dish | ṭaba' gāneby (m) | طبق جانبي |

| | | |
|---|---|---|
| spaghetti | spaɣetti (m) | سباجيتي |
| mash | baṭāṭes mahrūsa (f) | بطاطس مهروسة |
| pizza | bītza (f) | بيتزا |
| porridge (oatmeal, etc.) | ʿaṣīda (f) | عصيدة |
| omelette | omlette (m) | اومليت |
| | | |
| boiled (e.g. ~ beef) | maslūʾ | مسلوق |
| smoked (adj) | modakχen | مدخّن |
| fried (adj) | maʾly | مقلي |
| dried (adj) | mogaffaf | مجفّف |
| frozen (adj) | mogammad | مجمّد |
| pickled (adj) | meχallel | مخلّل |
| | | |
| sweet (sugary) | mesakkar | مسكّر |
| salty (adj) | māleḥ | مالح |
| cold (adj) | bāred | بارد |
| hot (adj) | soχn | سخن |
| bitter (adj) | morr | مرّ |
| tasty (adj) | ḥelw | حلو |
| | | |
| to cook in boiling water | salaʾ | سلق |
| to cook (dinner) | ḥaḍḍar | حضّر |
| to fry (vt) | ʾala | قلي |
| to heat up (food) | sakχan | سخّن |
| | | |
| to salt (vt) | rasʃ malḥ | رشّ ملح |
| to pepper (vt) | rasʃ felfel | رشّ فلفل |
| to grate (vt) | baraʃ | برش |
| peel (n) | ʾeʃra (f) | قشرة |
| to peel (vt) | ʾasʃar | قشّر |

## 52. Food

| | | |
|---|---|---|
| meat | laḥma (f) | لحمة |
| chicken | ferāχ (m) | فراخ |
| poussin | farrūg (m) | فرّوج |
| duck | baṭṭa (f) | بطّة |
| goose | wezza (f) | وزّة |
| game | ṣeyd (m) | صيد |
| turkey | dīk rūmy (m) | ديك رومي |
| | | |
| pork | laḥm el χanazīr (m) | لحم الخنزير |
| veal | laḥm el ʿegl (m) | لحم العجل |
| lamb | laḥm ḍāny (m) | لحم ضاني |
| beef | laḥm baqary (m) | لحم بقري |
| rabbit | laḥm arāneb (m) | لحم أرانب |
| | | |
| sausage (bologna, etc.) | sogoʾʾ (m) | سجق |
| vienna sausage (frankfurter) | sogoʾʾ (m) | سجق |
| bacon | bakon (m) | بيكون |
| ham | hām(m) | هام |
| gammon | faχd χanzīr (m) | فخد خنزير |
| pâté | maʿgūn laḥm (m) | معجون لحم |
| liver | kebda (f) | كبدة |

| | | |
|---|---|---|
| mince (minced meat) | hamburger (m) | هامبورجر |
| tongue | lesān (m) | لسان |
| egg | beyḍa (f) | بيضة |
| eggs | beyḍ (m) | بيض |
| egg white | bayāḍ el beyḍ (m) | بياض البيض |
| egg yolk | ṣafār el beyḍ (m) | صفار البيض |
| fish | samak (m) | سمك |
| seafood | sīfūd (pl) | سي فود |
| caviar | kaviar (m) | كافيار |
| crab | kaboria (m) | كابوريا |
| prawn | gammbary (m) | جمّبري |
| oyster | maḥār (m) | محار |
| spiny lobster | estakoza (m) | استاكوزا |
| octopus | aχṭabūṭ (m) | أخطبوط |
| squid | kalmāry (m) | كالماري |
| sturgeon | samak el ḥafʃ (m) | سمك الحفش |
| salmon | salamon (m) | سلمون |
| halibut | samak el halbūt (m) | سمك الهلبوت |
| cod | samak el qadd (m) | سمك القد |
| mackerel | makerel (m) | ماكريل |
| tuna | tuna (f) | تونة |
| eel | ḥankalīs (m) | حنكليس |
| trout | salamon mera''aṭ (m) | سلمون مرقّط |
| sardine | sardīn (m) | سردين |
| pike | samak el karāky (m) | سمك الكراكي |
| herring | renga (f) | رنجة |
| bread | ʿeyʃ (m) | عيش |
| cheese | gebna (f) | جبنة |
| sugar | sokkar (m) | سكّر |
| salt | melḥ (m) | ملح |
| rice | rozz (m) | رزّ |
| pasta (macaroni) | makaruna (f) | مكرونة |
| noodles | nūdles (f) | نودلز |
| butter | zebda (f) | زبدة |
| vegetable oil | zeyt (m) | زيت |
| sunflower oil | zeyt ʿabbād el ʃams (m) | زيت عبّاد الشمس |
| margarine | margarīn (m) | مارجرين |
| olives | zaytūn (m) | زيتون |
| olive oil | zeyt el zaytūn (m) | زيت الزيتون |
| milk | laban (m) | لبن |
| condensed milk | ḥalīb mokassaf (m) | حليب مكثّف |
| yogurt | zabādy (m) | زبادي |
| soured cream | kreyma ḥamḍa (f) | كريمة حامضة |
| cream (of milk) | krīma (f) | كريمة |
| mayonnaise | mayonnɛ:z (m) | مايونيز |

| | | |
|---|---|---|
| buttercream | krīmet zebda (f) | كريمة زبدة |
| groats (barley ~, etc.) | ḥobūb ʾamḥ (pl) | حبوب قمح |
| flour | deīʾ (m) | دقيق |
| tinned food | moʿallabāt (pl) | معلّبات |
| cornflakes | korn fleks (m) | كورن فليكس |
| honey | ʿasal (m) | عسل |
| jam | mrabba (m) | مربّى |
| chewing gum | lebān (m) | لبان |

## 53. Drinks

| | | |
|---|---|---|
| water | meyāh (f) | مياه |
| drinking water | mayet ʃorb (m) | ميّة شرب |
| mineral water | maya maʿdaniya (f) | ميّة معدنية |
| still (adj) | rakeda | راكدة |
| carbonated (adj) | kanz | كانز |
| sparkling (adj) | kanz | كانز |
| ice | talg (m) | ثلج |
| with ice | bel talg | بالتلج |
| non-alcoholic (adj) | men ɣeyr koḥūl | من غير كحول |
| soft drink | maʃrūb ɣāzy (m) | مشروب غازي |
| refreshing drink | ḥāga saʾʿa (f) | حاجة ساقعة |
| lemonade | limonāta (f) | ليموناتة |
| spirits | maʃrūbāt koḥūliya (pl) | مشروبات كحولية |
| wine | χamra (f) | خمرة |
| white wine | nebīz abyaḍ (m) | نبيذ أبيض |
| red wine | nebī aḥmar (m) | نبيذ أحمر |
| liqueur | liqure (m) | ليكيور |
| champagne | ʃambania (f) | شمبانيا |
| vermouth | vermote (m) | فيرموت |
| whisky | wiski (m) | ويسكي |
| vodka | vodka (f) | فودكا |
| gin | ʒin (m) | جين |
| cognac | konyāk (m) | كونياك |
| rum | rum (m) | رم |
| coffee | ʾahwa (f) | قهوة |
| black coffee | ʾahwa sāda (f) | قهوة سادة |
| white coffee | ʾahwa bel ḥalīb (f) | قهوة بالحليب |
| cappuccino | kaputʃino (m) | كابتشينو |
| instant coffee | neskafe (m) | نيسكافيه |
| milk | laban (m) | لبن |
| cocktail | koktayl (m) | كوكتيل |
| milkshake | milk ʃejk (m) | ميلك شيك |
| juice | ʿaṣīr (m) | عصير |
| tomato juice | ʿaṣīr ṭamāṭem (m) | عصير طماطم |

| | | |
|---|---|---|
| orange juice | ʻaṣīr bortoqāl (m) | عصير برتقال |
| freshly squeezed juice | ʻaṣīr freʃ (m) | عصير فريش |
| beer | bīra (f) | بيرة |
| lager | bīra χafīfa (f) | بيرة خفيفة |
| bitter | bīra ɣam'a (f) | بيرة غامقة |
| tea | ʃāy (m) | شاي |
| black tea | ʃāy aḥmar (m) | شاي أحمر |
| green tea | ʃāy aχḍar (m) | شاي أخضر |

## 54. Vegetables

| | | |
|---|---|---|
| vegetables | χoḍār (pl) | خضار |
| greens | χoḍrawāt waraqiya (pl) | خضروات ورقية |
| tomato | ṭamāṭem (f) | طماطم |
| cucumber | χeyār (m) | خيار |
| carrot | gazar (m) | جزر |
| potato | baṭāṭes (f) | بطاطس |
| onion | baṣal (m) | بصل |
| garlic | tūm (m) | ثوم |
| cabbage | koronb (m) | كرنب |
| cauliflower | 'arnabīṭ (m) | قرنبيط |
| Brussels sprouts | koronb broksel (m) | كرنب بروكسل |
| broccoli | brokkoli (m) | بركولي |
| beetroot | bangar (m) | بنجر |
| aubergine | bātengān (m) | باذنجان |
| courgette | kōsa (f) | كوسة |
| pumpkin | qarʻ ʻasaly (m) | قرع عسلي |
| turnip | left (m) | لفت |
| parsley | ba'dūnes (m) | بقدونس |
| dill | ʃabat (m) | شبت |
| lettuce | χass (m) | خسّ |
| celery | karfas (m) | كرفس |
| asparagus | helione (m) | هليون |
| spinach | sabāneχ (m) | سبانخ |
| pea | besella (f) | بسلّة |
| beans | fūl (m) | فول |
| maize | dora (f) | ذرة |
| kidney bean | faṣolya (f) | فاصوليا |
| sweet paper | felfel (m) | فلفل |
| radish | fegl (m) | فجل |
| artichoke | χarʃūf (m) | خرشوف |

## 55. Fruits. Nuts

| | | |
|---|---|---|
| fruit | faχa (f) | فاكهة |
| apple | toffāḥa (f) | تفّاحة |

| | | |
|---|---|---|
| pear | komettra (f) | كمّثرى |
| lemon | lymūn (m) | ليمون |
| orange | bortoqāl (m) | برتقال |
| strawberry (garden ~) | farawla (f) | فراولة |
| tangerine | yosfy (m) | يوسفي |
| plum | bar'ū' (m) | برقوق |
| peach | χawχa (f) | خوخة |
| apricot | meʃmeʃ (f) | مشمش |
| raspberry | tūt el 'alī' el aḥmar (m) | توت العليق الأحمر |
| pineapple | ananās (m) | أناناس |
| banana | moze (m) | موز |
| watermelon | baṭṭīχ (m) | بطّيخ |
| grape | 'enab (m) | عنب |
| cherry | karaz (m) | كرز |
| melon | ʃammām (f) | شمّام |
| grapefruit | grabe frūt (m) | جريب فروت |
| avocado | avokado (f) | افوكاتو |
| papaya | babāya (m) | ببايا |
| mango | manga (m) | مانجة |
| pomegranate | rommān (m) | رمان |
| redcurrant | keʃmeʃ aḥmar (m) | كشمش أحمر |
| blackcurrant | keʃmeʃ aswad (m) | كشمش أسود |
| gooseberry | 'enab el sa'lab (m) | عنب الثعلب |
| bilberry | 'enab al aḥrāg (m) | عنب الأحراج |
| blackberry | tūt aswad (m) | توت أسود |
| raisin | zebīb (m) | زبيب |
| fig | tīn (m) | تين |
| date | tamr (m) | تمر |
| peanut | fūl sudāny (m) | فول سوداني |
| almond | loze (m) | لوز |
| walnut | 'eyn gamal (f) | عين الجمل |
| hazelnut | bondo' (m) | بندق |
| coconut | goze el hend (m) | جوز هند |
| pistachios | fosto' (m) | فستق |

## 56. Bread. Sweets

| | | |
|---|---|---|
| bakers' confectionery (pastry) | ḥalawīāt (pl) | حلويّات |
| bread | 'eyʃ (m) | عيش |
| biscuits | baskawīt (m) | بسكويت |
| chocolate (n) | ʃokolāta (f) | شكولاتة |
| chocolate (as adj) | bel ʃokolāṭa | بالشكولاتة |
| candy (wrapped) | bonbony (m) | بونبوني |
| cake (e.g. cupcake) | keyka (f) | كيكة |
| cake (e.g. birthday ~) | torta (f) | تورتة |
| pie (e.g. apple ~) | feṭīra (f) | فطيرة |
| filling (for cake, pie) | ḥaʃwa (f) | حشوة |

| | | |
|---|---|---|
| jam (whole fruit jam) | mrabba (m) | مربّى |
| marmalade | marmalād (f) | مرملاد |
| wafers | waffles (pl) | وافلز |
| ice-cream | 'ays krīm (m) | آيس كريم |
| pudding (Christmas ~) | būding (m) | بودنج |

## 57. Spices

| | | |
|---|---|---|
| salt | melḥ (m) | ملح |
| salty (adj) | māleḥ | مالِح |
| to salt (vt) | rasʃ malḥ | رش ملح |
| black pepper | felfel aswad (m) | فلفل أسوّد |
| red pepper (milled ~) | felfel aḥmar (m) | فلفل أحمر |
| mustard | mosṭarda (m) | مسطردة |
| horseradish | fegl ḥār (m) | فجل حار |
| condiment | bahār (m) | بهار |
| spice | bahār (m) | بهار |
| sauce | ṣalṣa (f) | صلصة |
| vinegar | χall (m) | خلّ |
| anise | yansūn (m) | ينسون |
| basil | rīḥān (m) | ريحان |
| cloves | 'oronfol (m) | قرنفل |
| ginger | zangabīl (m) | زنجبيل |
| coriander | kozbora (f) | كزبرة |
| cinnamon | 'erfa (f) | قرفة |
| sesame | semsem (m) | سمسم |
| bay leaf | wara' el ɣār (m) | ورق الغار |
| paprika | babrika (f) | بابريكا |
| caraway | karawya (f) | كراوية |
| saffron | zaʕfarān (m) | زعفران |

# PERSONAL INFORMATION. FAMILY

## 58. Personal information. Forms

| | | |
|---|---|---|
| name (first name) | esm (m) | اسم |
| surname (last name) | esm el ʿa'ela (m) | اسم العائلة |
| date of birth | tarīχ el melād (m) | تاريخ الميلاد |
| place of birth | makān el melād (m) | مكان الميلاد |
| nationality | gensiya (f) | جنسيّة |
| place of residence | maqarr el eqāma (m) | مقرّ الإقامة |
| country | balad (m) | بلد |
| profession (occupation) | mehna (f) | مهنة |
| gender, sex | ginss (m) | جنس |
| height | ṭūl (m) | طول |
| weight | wazn (m) | وزن |

## 59. Family members. Relatives

| | | |
|---|---|---|
| mother | walda (f) | والدة |
| father | wāled (m) | والد |
| son | walad (m) | ولد |
| daughter | bent (f) | بنت |
| younger daughter | el bent el saɣīra (f) | البنت الصغيرة |
| younger son | el ebn el saɣīr (m) | الابن الصغير |
| eldest daughter | el bent el kebīra (f) | البنت الكبيرة |
| eldest son | el ebn el kabīr (m) | الابن الكبير |
| brother | aχ (m) | أخ |
| elder brother | el aχ el kibīr (m) | الأخ الكبير |
| younger brother | el aχ el ṣoɣeyyir (m) | الأخ الصغير |
| sister | uχt (f) | أخت |
| elder sister | el uχt el kibīra (f) | الأخت الكبيرة |
| younger sister | el uχt el ṣoɣeyyira (f) | الأخت الصغيرة |
| cousin (masc.) | ibn ʿamm (m), ibn χāl (m) | إبن عمّ, إبن خال |
| cousin (fem.) | bint ʿamm (f), bint χāl (f) | بنت عمّ, بنت خال |
| mummy | mama (f) | ماما |
| dad, daddy | baba (m) | بابا |
| parents | waldeyn (du) | والدين |
| child | ṭefl (m) | طفل |
| children | aṭfāl (pl) | أطفال |
| grandmother | gedda (f) | جدّة |
| grandfather | gadd (m) | جدّ |
| grandson | ḥafīd (m) | حفيد |

| | | |
|---|---|---|
| granddaughter | ḥafīda (f) | حفيدة |
| grandchildren | aḥfād (pl) | أحفاد |
| uncle | ʿamm (m), χāl (m) | عمّ, خال |
| aunt | ʿamma (f), χāla (f) | عمة, خالة |
| nephew | ibn el aχ (m), ibn el uχt (m) | إبن الأخ, إبن الأخت |
| niece | bint el aχ (f), bint el uχt (f) | بنت الأخ, بنت الأخت |
| mother-in-law (wife's mother) | ḥamah (f) | حماة |
| father-in-law (husband's father) | ḥama (m) | حما |
| son-in-law (daughter's husband) | goze el bent (m) | جوز البنت |
| stepmother | merāt el abb (f) | مرات الأب |
| stepfather | goze el omm (m) | جوز الأم |
| infant | ṭefl raḍeeʿ (m) | طفل رضيع |
| baby (infant) | mawlūd (m) | موّلود |
| little boy, kid | walad ṣaɣīr (m) | ولد صغير |
| wife | goza (f) | جوزة |
| husband | goze (m) | جوز |
| spouse (husband) | goze (m) | جوز |
| spouse (wife) | goza (f) | جوزة |
| married (masc.) | metgawwez | متجوّز |
| married (fem.) | metgawweza | متجوّزة |
| single (unmarried) | aʿzab | أعزب |
| bachelor | aʿzab (m) | أعزب |
| divorced (masc.) | moṭallaq (m) | مطلّق |
| widow | armala (f) | أرملة |
| widower | armal (m) | أرمل |
| relative | ʾarīb (m) | قريب |
| close relative | nesīb ʾarīb (m) | نسيب قريب |
| distant relative | nesīb beʿīd (m) | نسيب بعيد |
| relatives | aqāreb (pl) | أقارب |
| orphan (boy or girl) | yatīm (m) | يتيم |
| guardian (of a minor) | walyī amr (m) | وليّ أمر |
| to adopt (a boy) | tabanna | تبنّى |
| to adopt (a girl) | tabanna | تبنّى |

## 60. Friends. Colleagues

| | | |
|---|---|---|
| friend (masc.) | ṣadīq (m) | صديق |
| friend (fem.) | ṣadīqa (f) | صديقة |
| friendship | ṣadāqa (f) | صداقة |
| to be friends | ṣādaq | صادق |
| pal (masc.) | ṣāḥeb (m) | صاحب |
| pal (fem.) | ṣaḥba (f) | صاحبة |
| partner | rafīʾ (m) | رفيق |
| chief (boss) | raʾīs (m) | رئيس |

| | | |
|---|---|---|
| superior (n) | el arfaʿ maqāman (m) | الأرفع مقاماً |
| owner, proprietor | ṣāḥib (m) | صاحب |
| subordinate (n) | tābeʿ (m) | تابع |
| colleague | zamīl (m) | زميل |
| | | |
| acquaintance (person) | maʿrefa (m) | معرفة |
| fellow traveller | rafīʾ safar (m) | رفيق سفر |
| classmate | zamīl fel ṣaff (m) | زميل في الصفّ |
| | | |
| neighbour (masc.) | gār (m) | جار |
| neighbour (fem.) | gāra (f) | جارة |
| neighbours | gerān (pl) | جيران |

# HUMAN BODY. MEDICINE

## 61. Head

| | | |
|---|---|---|
| head | ra's (m) | رأس |
| face | weʃ (m) | وش |
| nose | manaχīr (m) | مناخير |
| mouth | bo' (m) | بوء |
| eye | ʿeyn (f) | عين |
| eyes | ʿoyūn (pl) | عيون |
| pupil | ḥad'a (f) | حدقة |
| eyebrow | ḥāgeb (m) | حاجب |
| eyelash | remʃ (m) | رمش |
| eyelid | gefn (m) | جفن |
| tongue | lesān (m) | لسان |
| tooth | senna (f) | سنّة |
| lips | ʃafāyef (pl) | شفايف |
| cheekbones | ʿaḍmet el χadd (f) | عضمة الخدّ |
| gum | lassa (f) | لثّة |
| palate | ḥanak (m) | حنك |
| nostrils | manaχer (pl) | مناخر |
| chin | da''n (m) | دقن |
| jaw | fakk (m) | فكّ |
| cheek | χadd (m) | خدّ |
| forehead | gabha (f) | جبهة |
| temple | ṣedɣ (m) | صدغ |
| ear | wedn (f) | ودن |
| back of the head | 'afa (m) | قفا |
| neck | ra'aba (f) | رقبة |
| throat | zore (m) | زور |
| hair | ʃaʿr (m) | شعر |
| hairstyle | tasrīḥa (f) | تسريحة |
| haircut | tasrīḥa (f) | تسريحة |
| wig | barūka (f) | باروكة |
| moustache | ʃanab (pl) | شنب |
| beard | leḥya (f) | لحية |
| to have (a beard, etc.) | ʿando | عنده |
| plait | ḍefīra (f) | ضفيرة |
| sideboards | sawālef (pl) | سوالف |
| red-haired (adj) | aḥmar el ʃaʿr | أحمر الشعر |
| grey (hair) | ʃaʿr abyaḍ | شعر أبيض |
| bald (adj) | aṣlaʿ | أصلع |
| bald patch | ṣalaʿ (m) | صلع |

| | | |
|---|---|---|
| ponytail | deyl ḥoṣān (m) | ديل حصان |
| fringe | ʾoṣṣa (f) | قصّة |

## 62. Human body

| | | |
|---|---|---|
| hand | yad (m) | يد |
| arm | derāʿ (f) | دراع |
| finger | ṣobāʿ (m) | صباع |
| toe | ṣobāʿ el ʾadam (m) | صباع القدم |
| thumb | ebhām (m) | إبهام |
| little finger | χonṣor (m) | خنصر |
| nail | ḍefr (m) | ضفر |
| fist | qabḍa (f) | قبضة |
| palm | kaff (f) | كفّ |
| wrist | meʿṣam (m) | معصم |
| forearm | sāʿed (m) | ساعد |
| elbow | kūʿ (m) | كوع |
| shoulder | ketf (f) | كتف |
| leg | regl (f) | رجل |
| foot | qadam (f) | قدم |
| knee | rokba (f) | ركبة |
| calf | semmāna (f) | سمّانة |
| hip | faχd (f) | فخد |
| heel | kaʿb (m) | كعب |
| body | gesm (m) | جسم |
| stomach | baṭn (m) | بطن |
| chest | ṣedr (m) | صدر |
| breast | sady (m) | ثدي |
| flank | ganb (m) | جنب |
| back | ḍahr (m) | ضهر |
| lower back | asfal el ḍahr (m) | أسفل الضهر |
| waist | wesṭ (f) | وسط |
| navel (belly button) | sorra (f) | سرّة |
| buttocks | ardāf (pl) | أرداف |
| bottom | debr (m) | دبر |
| beauty spot | ʃāma (f) | شامة |
| birthmark (café au lait spot) | waḥma | وحمة |
| tattoo | waʃm (m) | وشم |
| scar | nadba (f) | ندبة |

## 63. Diseases

| | | |
|---|---|---|
| illness | maraḍ (m) | مرض |
| to be ill | mereḍ | مرض |
| health | ṣeḥḥa (f) | صحّة |
| runny nose (coryza) | raʃ-ḥ fel anf (m) | رشح في الأنف |

| | | |
|---|---|---|
| tonsillitis | eltehāb el lawzateyn (m) | إلتهاب اللوزتين |
| cold (illness) | zokām (m) | زكام |
| to catch a cold | gālo bard | جاله برد |
| bronchitis | eltehāb ʃoʿaby (m) | إلتهاب شعبيّ |
| pneumonia | eltehāb raʾawy (m) | إلتهاب رئوي |
| flu, influenza | influenza (f) | إنفلونزا |
| shortsighted (adj) | ʾaṣīr el naẓar | قصير النظر |
| longsighted (adj) | beʿīd el naẓar | بعيد النظر |
| strabismus (crossed eyes) | ḥawal (m) | حوَل |
| squint-eyed (adj) | aḥwal | أحوَل |
| cataract | katarakt (f) | كاتاراكت |
| glaucoma | glawkoma (f) | جلوكوما |
| stroke | sakta (f) | سكتة |
| heart attack | azma ʾalbiya (f) | أزمة قلبية |
| myocardial infarction | nawba ʾalbiya (f) | نوبة قلبية |
| paralysis | ʃalal (m) | شلل |
| to paralyse (vt) | ʃall | شلّ |
| allergy | ḥasasiya (f) | حساسيّة |
| asthma | rabw (m) | ربو |
| diabetes | dāʾ el sokkary (m) | داء السكّري |
| toothache | alam asnān (m) | ألم الأسنان |
| caries | naχr el asnān (m) | نخر الأسنان |
| diarrhoea | es-hāl (m) | إسهال |
| constipation | emsāk (m) | إمساك |
| stomach upset | eḍṭrāb el meʿda (m) | إضطراب المعدة |
| food poisoning | tasammom (m) | تسمم |
| to get food poisoning | etsammem | إتسمّم |
| arthritis | eltehāb el mafāṣel (m) | إلتهاب المفاصل |
| rickets | kosāḥ el aṭfāl (m) | كساح الأطفال |
| rheumatism | rheumatism (m) | روماتزم |
| atherosclerosis | taṣṣallob el ʃarayīn (m) | تصلّب الشرايين |
| gastritis | eltehāb el meʿda (m) | إلتهاب المعدة |
| appendicitis | eltehāb el zayda el dūdiya (m) | إلتهاب الزائدة الدودية |
| cholecystitis | eltehāb el marāra (m) | إلتهاب المرارة |
| ulcer | qorḥa (f) | قرحة |
| measles | maraḍ el ḥaṣba (m) | مرض الحصبة |
| rubella (German measles) | el ḥaṣba el almaniya (f) | الحصبة الألمانية |
| jaundice | yaraqān (m) | يرقان |
| hepatitis | eltehāb el kabed el vayrūsy (m) | إلتهاب الكبد الفيروسي |
| schizophrenia | fuṣām (m) | فصام |
| rabies (hydrophobia) | dāʾ el kalb (m) | داء الكلب |
| neurosis | eḍṭrāb ʿaṣaby (m) | إضطراب عصبي |
| concussion | ertegāg el moχ (m) | إرتجاج المخ |
| cancer | saraṭān (m) | سرطان |
| sclerosis | taṣṣallob (m) | تصلّب |

| | | |
|---|---|---|
| multiple sclerosis | taṣṣallob mota'added (m) | تصلّب متعدّد |
| alcoholism | edmān el χamr (m) | إدمان الخمر |
| alcoholic (n) | modmen el χamr (m) | مدمن الخمر |
| syphilis | syfilis el zehry (m) | سفلس الزهري |
| AIDS | el eydz (m) | الايدز |
| tumour | waram (m) | ورم |
| malignant (adj) | χabīs | خبيث |
| benign (adj) | ḥamīd (m) | حميد |
| fever | ḥomma (f) | حمّى |
| malaria | malaria (f) | ملاريا |
| gangrene | ɣanɣarīna (f) | غنغرينا |
| seasickness | dawār el baḥr (m) | دوار البحر |
| epilepsy | maraḍ el ṣara' (m) | مرض الصرع |
| epidemic | wabā' (m) | وباء |
| typhus | tyfus (m) | تيفوس |
| tuberculosis | maraḍ el soll (m) | مرض السلّ |
| cholera | kōlīra (f) | كوليرا |
| plague (bubonic ~) | ṭa'ūn (m) | طاعون |

## 64. Symptoms. Treatments. Part 1

| | | |
|---|---|---|
| symptom | 'araḍ (m) | عرض |
| temperature | ḥarāra (f) | حرارة |
| high temperature (fever) | ḥomma (f) | حمّى |
| pulse (heartbeat) | nabḍ (m) | نبض |
| dizziness (vertigo) | dawχa (f) | دوخة |
| hot (adj) | soχn | سخن |
| shivering | ra'ʃa (f) | رعشة |
| pale (e.g. ~ face) | aṣfar | أصفر |
| cough | koḥḥa (f) | كحّة |
| to cough (vi) | kaḥḥ | كحّ |
| to sneeze (vi) | 'aṭas | عطس |
| faint | dawχa (f) | دوخة |
| to faint (vi) | oɣma 'aleyh | أغمي عليه |
| bruise (hématome) | kadma (f) | كدمة |
| bump (lump) | tawarrom (m) | تورّم |
| to bang (bump) | etχabaṭ | إتخبط |
| contusion (bruise) | raḍḍa (f) | رضّة |
| to get a bruise | etkadam | إتكدم |
| to limp (vi) | 'arag | عرج |
| dislocation | χal' (m) | خلع |
| to dislocate (vt) | χala' | خلع |
| fracture | kasr (m) | كسر |
| to have a fracture | enkasar | إنكسر |
| cut (e.g. paper ~) | garḥ (m) | جرح |
| to cut oneself | garaḥ nafsoh | جرح نفسه |

| | | |
|---|---|---|
| bleeding | nazīf (m) | نزيف |
| burn (injury) | ḥar' (m) | حرق |
| to get burned | et-ḥara' | إتحرق |
| to prick (vt) | waχaz | وخز |
| to prick oneself | waχaz nafso | وخز نفسه |
| to injure (vt) | aṣāb | أصاب |
| injury | eṣāba (f) | إصابة |
| wound | garḥ (m) | جرح |
| trauma | ṣadma (f) | صدمة |
| to be delirious | haza | هذى |
| to stutter (vi) | tala'sam | تلعثم |
| sunstroke | ḍarabet ʃams (f) | ضربة شمس |

## 65. Symptoms. Treatments. Part 2

| | | |
|---|---|---|
| pain, ache | alam (m) | ألم |
| splinter (in foot, etc.) | ʃazya (f) | شظية |
| sweat (perspiration) | 'er' (m) | عرق |
| to sweat (perspire) | 'ere' | عرق |
| vomiting | targee' (m) | ترجيع |
| convulsions | taʃonnogāt (pl) | تشنّجات |
| pregnant (adj) | ḥāmel | حامل |
| to be born | etwalad | اتولّد |
| delivery, labour | welāda (f) | ولادة |
| to deliver (~ a baby) | walad | ولد |
| abortion | eg-hāḍ (m) | إجهاض |
| breathing, respiration | tanaffos (m) | تنفّس |
| in-breath (inhalation) | estenʃāq (m) | إستنشاق |
| out-breath (exhalation) | zafīr (m) | زفير |
| to exhale (breathe out) | zafar | زفر |
| to inhale (vi) | estanʃaq | إستنشق |
| disabled person | mo'āq (m) | معاق |
| cripple | moq'ad (m) | مقعد |
| drug addict | modmen moχaddarāt (m) | مدمن مخدّرات |
| deaf (adj) | aṭraʃ | أطرش |
| mute (adj) | aχras | أخرس |
| deaf mute (adj) | aṭraʃ aχras | أطرش أخرس |
| mad, insane (adj) | magnūn | مجنون |
| madman (demented person) | magnūn (m) | مجنون |
| madwoman | magnūna (f) | مجنونة |
| to go insane | etgannen | اتجنّن |
| gene | ʒīn (m) | جين |
| immunity | manā'a (f) | مناعة |
| hereditary (adj) | werāsy | وراثي |

| | | |
|---|---|---|
| congenital (adj) | χolqy men el welāda | خلقي من الولادة |
| virus | virūs (m) | فيروس |
| microbe | mikrūb (m) | ميكروب |
| bacterium | garsūma (f) | جرثومة |
| infection | ʿadwa (f) | عدوى |

## 66. Symptoms. Treatments. Part 3

| | | |
|---|---|---|
| hospital | mostaʃfa (m) | مستشفى |
| patient | marīḍ (m) | مريض |
| | | |
| diagnosis | taʃχīṣ (m) | تشخيص |
| cure | ʃefāʾ (m) | شفاء |
| medical treatment | ʿelāg ṭebby (m) | علاج طبي |
| to get treatment | etʿāleg | اتعالج |
| to treat (~ a patient) | ʿālag | عالج |
| to nurse (look after) | marraḍ | مرّض |
| care (nursing ~) | ʿenāya (f) | عناية |
| | | |
| operation, surgery | ʿamaliya grāḥiya (f) | عمليّة جراحية |
| to bandage (head, limb) | ḍammad | ضمّد |
| bandaging | taḍmīd (m) | تضميد |
| | | |
| vaccination | talqīḥ (m) | تلقيح |
| to vaccinate (vt) | laqqaḥ | لقّح |
| injection | ḥoʾna (f) | حقنة |
| to give an injection | ḥaʾan ebra | حقن إبرة |
| | | |
| attack | nawba (f) | نوبة |
| amputation | batr (m) | بتر |
| to amputate (vt) | batr | بتر |
| coma | ɣaybūba (f) | غيبوبة |
| to be in a coma | kān fi ḥālet ɣaybūba | كان في حالة غيبوبة |
| intensive care | el ʿenāya el morakkaza (f) | العناية المركّزة |
| | | |
| to recover (~ from flu) | ʃefy | شفي |
| condition (patient's ~) | ḥāla (f) | حالة |
| consciousness | waʿy (m) | وعي |
| memory (faculty) | zākera (f) | ذاكرة |
| | | |
| to pull out (tooth) | χalaʿ | خلع |
| filling | ḥaʃww (m) | حشوّ |
| to fill (a tooth) | ḥaʃa | حشا |
| | | |
| hypnosis | el tanwīm el meɣnaṭīsy (m) | التنويم المغناطيسى |
| to hypnotize (vt) | nawwem | نوّم |

## 67. Medicine. Drugs. Accessories

| | | |
|---|---|---|
| medicine, drug | dawāʾ (m) | دواء |
| remedy | ʿelāg (m) | علاج |
| to prescribe (vt) | waṣaf | وصف |

| | | |
|---|---|---|
| prescription | waṣfa (f) | وصفة |
| tablet, pill | 'orṣ (m) | قرص |
| ointment | marham (m) | مرهم |
| ampoule | ambūla (f) | أمبولة |
| mixture, solution | dawā' ʃorb (m) | دواء شراب |
| syrup | ʃarāb (m) | شراب |
| capsule | ḥabba (f) | حبّة |
| powder | zorūr (m) | ذرور |
| gauze bandage | ḍammāda ʃāʃ (f) | ضمادة شاش |
| cotton wool | 'oṭn (m) | قطن |
| iodine | yūd (m) | يود |
| plaster | blaster (m) | بلاستر |
| eyedropper | 'aṭṭāra (f) | قطّارة |
| thermometer | termometr (m) | ترمومتر |
| syringe | serennga (f) | سرنجة |
| wheelchair | korsy motaḥarrek (m) | كرسي متحرك |
| crutches | 'okkāz (m) | عكّاز |
| painkiller | mosakken (m) | مسكّن |
| laxative | molayen (m) | مليّن |
| spirits (ethanol) | etanol (m) | إيثانول |
| medicinal herbs | a'ʃāb ṭebbiya (pl) | أعشاب طبّية |
| herbal (~ tea) | 'oʃby | عشبي |

# FLAT

## 68. Flat

| | | |
|---|---|---|
| flat | ʃa''a (f) | شقّة |
| room | oḍa (f) | أوضة |
| bedroom | oḍet el nome (f) | أوضة النوم |
| dining room | oḍet el sofra (f) | أوضة السفرة |
| living room | oḍet el esteqbāl (f) | أوضة الإستقبال |
| study (home office) | maktab (m) | مكتب |
| entry room | madχal (m) | مدخل |
| bathroom | ḥammām (m) | حمّام |
| water closet | ḥammām (m) | حمّام |
| ceiling | sa'f (m) | سقف |
| floor | arḍiya (f) | أرضية |
| corner | zawya (f) | زاوية |

## 69. Furniture. Interior

| | | |
|---|---|---|
| furniture | asās (m) | أثاث |
| table | maktab (m) | مكتب |
| chair | korsy (m) | كرسي |
| bed | serīr (m) | سرير |
| sofa, settee | kanaba (f) | كنبة |
| armchair | korsy (m) | كرسي |
| bookcase | χazzānet kotob (f) | خزّانة كتب |
| shelf | raff (m) | رفّ |
| wardrobe | dolāb (m) | دولاب |
| coat rack (wall-mounted ~) | ʃammāʿa (f) | شمّاعة |
| coat stand | ʃammāʿa (f) | شمّاعة |
| chest of drawers | dolāb adrāg (m) | دولاب أدراج |
| coffee table | ṭarabeyzet el 'ahwa (f) | طرابيزة القهوة |
| mirror | merāya (f) | مراية |
| carpet | seggāda (f) | سجّادة |
| small carpet | seggāda (f) | سجّادة |
| fireplace | daffāya (f) | دفّاية |
| candle | ʃamʿa (f) | شمعة |
| candlestick | ʃamʿadān (m) | شمعدان |
| drapes | satā'er (pl) | ستائر |
| wallpaper | wara' ḥā'eṭ (m) | ورق حائط |

| | | |
|---|---|---|
| blinds (jalousie) | satā'er ofoqiya (pl) | ستائر أفقيّة |
| table lamp | abāʒūr (f) | اباجورة |
| wall lamp (sconce) | lammbet ḥā'eṭ (f) | لمّبة حائط |
| standard lamp | meṣbāḥ arḍy (m) | مصباح أرضي |
| chandelier | nagafa (f) | نجفة |
| leg (of a chair, table) | regl (f) | رجل |
| armrest | masnad (m) | مسند |
| back (backrest) | masnad (m) | مسند |
| drawer | dorg (m) | درج |

## 70. Bedding

| | | |
|---|---|---|
| bedclothes | bayāḍāt el serīr (pl) | بياضات السرير |
| pillow | maχadda (f) | مخدّة |
| pillowslip | kīs el maχadda (m) | كيس المخدّة |
| duvet | leḥāf (m) | لحاف |
| sheet | melāya (f) | ملاية |
| bedspread | ɣaṭā' el serīr (m) | غطاء السرير |

## 71. Kitchen

| | | |
|---|---|---|
| kitchen | maṭbaχ (m) | مطبخ |
| gas | ɣāz (m) | غاز |
| gas cooker | botoɣāz (m) | بوتوغاز |
| electric cooker | forn kaharabā'y (m) | فرن كهربائي |
| oven | forn (m) | فرن |
| microwave oven | mikroweyv (m) | ميكروويف |
| refrigerator | tallāga (f) | ثلاجة |
| freezer | freyzer (m) | فريزر |
| dishwasher | ɣassālet aṭbā' (f) | غسّالة أطباق |
| mincer | farrāmet laḥm (f) | فرّامة لحم |
| juicer | 'aṣṣāra (f) | عصّارة |
| toaster | maḥmaṣet χobz (f) | محمصة خبز |
| mixer | χallāṭ (m) | خلّاط |
| coffee machine | makinet ṣon' el 'ahwa (f) | ماكينة صنع القهوة |
| coffee pot | ɣallāya kahraba'iya (f) | غلّاية القهوة |
| coffee grinder | maṭ-ḥanet 'ahwa (f) | مطحنة قهوة |
| kettle | ɣallāya (f) | غلّاية |
| teapot | barrād el ʃāy (m) | برّاد الشاي |
| lid | ɣaṭā' (m) | غطاء |
| tea strainer | maṣfāh el ʃāy (f) | مصفاة الشاي |
| spoon | ma'la'a (f) | معلقة |
| teaspoon | ma'la'et ʃāy (f) | معلقة شاي |
| soup spoon | ma'la'a kebīra (f) | ملعقة كبيرة |
| fork | ʃawka (f) | شوكة |
| knife | sekkīna (f) | سكّينة |

| | | |
|---|---|---|
| tableware (dishes) | awāny (pl) | أواني |
| plate (dinner ~) | ṭaba' (m) | طبق |
| saucer | ṭaba' fengān (m) | طبق فنجان |
| shot glass | kāsa (f) | كاسة |
| glass (tumbler) | kobbāya (f) | كوبّاية |
| cup | fengān (m) | فنجان |
| sugar bowl | sokkariya (f) | سكّريّة |
| salt cellar | mamlaḥa (f) | مملحة |
| pepper pot | mobhera (f) | مبهرة |
| butter dish | ṭaba' zebda (m) | طبق زبدة |
| stock pot (soup pot) | ḥalla (f) | حلّة |
| frying pan (skillet) | ṭāsa (f) | طاسة |
| ladle | maɣrafa (f) | مغرفة |
| colander | maṣfāh (f) | مصفاه |
| tray (serving ~) | ṣeniya (f) | صينيّة |
| bottle | ezāza (f) | إزازة |
| jar (glass) | barṭamān (m) | برطمان |
| tin (can) | kanz (m) | كانز |
| bottle opener | fattāḥa (f) | فتّاحة |
| tin opener | fattāḥa (f) | فتّاحة |
| corkscrew | barrīma (f) | بريّمة |
| filter | filter (m) | فلتر |
| to filter (vt) | ṣaffa | صفّى |
| waste (food ~, etc.) | zebāla (f) | زبالة |
| waste bin (kitchen ~) | ṣandū' el zebāla (m) | صندوق الزبالة |

## 72. Bathroom

| | | |
|---|---|---|
| bathroom | ḥammām (m) | حمّام |
| water | meyāh (f) | مياه |
| tap | ḥanafiya (f) | حنفيّة |
| hot water | maya soxna (f) | مايّة سخنة |
| cold water | maya barda (f) | مايّة باردة |
| toothpaste | ma'gūn asnān (m) | معجون أسنان |
| to clean one's teeth | naḍḍaf el asnān | نظّف الأسنان |
| toothbrush | forʃet senān (f) | فرشة أسنان |
| to shave (vi) | ḥala' | حلق |
| shaving foam | raɣwa lel ḥelā'a (f) | رغوة للحلاقة |
| razor | mūs (m) | موس |
| to wash (one's hands, etc.) | ɣasal | غسل |
| to have a bath | estaḥamma | إستحمّى |
| shower | doʃ (m) | دوش |
| to have a shower | axad doʃ | أخد دوش |
| bath | banyo (m) | بانيو |
| toilet (toilet bowl) | twalet (m) | تواليت |

| | | |
|---|---|---|
| sink (washbasin) | ḥoḍe (m) | حوض |
| soap | ṣabūn (m) | صابون |
| soap dish | ṣabbāna (f) | صبّانة |
| sponge | līfa (f) | ليفة |
| shampoo | ʃambū (m) | شامبو |
| towel | fūṭa (f) | فوطة |
| bathrobe | robe el ḥammām (m) | روب حمّام |
| laundry (laundering) | ɣasīl (m) | غسيل |
| washing machine | ɣassāla (f) | غسّالة |
| to do the laundry | ɣasal el malābes | غسل الملابس |
| washing powder | mas-ḥūʾ ɣasīl (m) | مسحوق غسيل |

## 73. Household appliances

| | | |
|---|---|---|
| TV, telly | televizion (m) | تليفزيون |
| tape recorder | gehāz tasgīl (m) | جهاز تسجيل |
| video | ʾāla tasgīl video (f) | آلة تسجيل فيديو |
| radio | gehāz radio (m) | جهاز راديو |
| player (CD, MP3, etc.) | blayer (m) | بليير |
| video projector | gehāz ʿarḍ (m) | جهاز عرض |
| home cinema | sinema manzeliya (f) | سينما منزليّة |
| DVD player | dividī blayer (m) | دي في دي بليير |
| amplifier | mokabbaer el ṣote (m) | مكبّر الصوت |
| video game console | ʾātāry (m) | أتاري |
| video camera | kamera video (f) | كاميرا فيديو |
| camera (photo) | kamera (f) | كاميرا |
| digital camera | kamera diʒital (f) | كاميرا ديجيتال |
| vacuum cleaner | maknasa kahrabaʾiya (f) | مكنسة كهربائيّة |
| iron (e.g. steam ~) | makwa (f) | مكواة |
| ironing board | lawḥet kayī (f) | لوحة كيّ |
| telephone | telefon (m) | تليفون |
| mobile phone | mobile (m) | موبايل |
| typewriter | ʾāla katba (f) | آلة كاتبة |
| sewing machine | makanet el χeyāṭa (f) | مكنة الخياطة |
| microphone | mikrofon (m) | ميكروفون |
| headphones | sammaʿāt raʾsiya (pl) | سمّاعات رأسية |
| remote control (TV) | remowt kontrol (m) | ريموت كنترول |
| CD, compact disc | sidī (m) | سي دي |
| cassette, tape | kasett (m) | كاسيت |
| vinyl record | esṭewāna mūsīqa (f) | أسطوانة موسيقى |

# THE EARTH. WEATHER

## 74. Outer space

| | | |
|---|---|---|
| space | faḍā' (m) | فضاء |
| space (as adj) | faḍā'y | فضائي |
| outer space | el faḍā' el χāregy (m) | الفضاء الخارجي |
| world | 'ālam (m) | عالم |
| universe | el kōn (m) | الكون |
| galaxy | el magarra (f) | المجرّة |
| star | negm (m) | نجم |
| constellation | borg (m) | برج |
| planet | kawwkab (m) | كوكب |
| satellite | 'amar ṣenā'y (m) | قمر صناعي |
| meteorite | nayzek (m) | نيّزك |
| comet | mozannab (m) | مذنّب |
| asteroid | kowaykeb (m) | كويكب |
| orbit | madār (m) | مدار |
| to revolve (~ around the Earth) | dār | دار |
| atmosphere | el ɣelāf el gawwy (m) | الغلاف الجوّي |
| the Sun | el ʃams (f) | الشمس |
| solar system | el magmū'a el ʃamsiya (f) | المجموعة الشمسيّة |
| solar eclipse | kosūf el ʃams (m) | كسوف الشمس |
| the Earth | el arḍ (f) | الأرض |
| the Moon | el 'amar (m) | القمر |
| Mars | el marrīχ (m) | المرّيخ |
| Venus | el zahra (f) | الزهرة |
| Jupiter | el moʃtary (m) | المشتري |
| Saturn | zoḥḥol (m) | زحل |
| Mercury | 'aṭāred (m) | عطارد |
| Uranus | uranus (m) | اورانوس |
| Neptune | nibtūn (m) | نبتون |
| Pluto | bluto (m) | بلوتو |
| Milky Way | darb el tebbāna (m) | درب التبّانة |
| Great Bear (Ursa Major) | el dobb el akbar (m) | الدب الأكبر |
| North Star | negm el 'oṭb (m) | نجم القطب |
| Martian | sāken el marrīχ (m) | ساكن المرّيخ |
| extraterrestrial (n) | faḍā'y (m) | فضائي |
| alien | kā'en faḍā'y (m) | كائن فضائي |

| | | |
|---|---|---|
| flying saucer | ṭaba' ṭā'er (m) | طبق طائر |
| spaceship | markaba faḍa'iya (f) | مركبة فضائية |
| space station | maḥaṭṭet faḍā' (f) | محطّة فضاء |
| blast-off | enṭelāq (m) | إنطلاق |
| engine | motore (m) | موتور |
| nozzle | manfaθ (m) | منفث |
| fuel | woqūd (m) | وقود |
| cockpit, flight deck | kabīna (f) | كابينة |
| aerial | hawā'y (m) | هوائي |
| porthole | kowwa mostadīra (f) | كوّة مستديرة |
| solar panel | lawḥa ʃamsiya (f) | لوحة شمسيّة |
| spacesuit | badlet el faḍā' (f) | بدّلة الفضاء |
| weightlessness | enʿedām wazn (m) | إنعدام الوزن |
| oxygen | oksiʒīn (m) | أوكسجين |
| docking (in space) | rasw (m) | رسو |
| to dock (vi, vt) | rasa | رسى |
| observatory | marṣad (m) | مرصد |
| telescope | teleskop (m) | تلسكوب |
| to observe (vt) | rāqab | راقب |
| to explore (vt) | estakʃef | إستكشف |

## 75. The Earth

| | | |
|---|---|---|
| the Earth | el arḍ (f) | الأرض |
| the globe (the Earth) | el kora el arḍiya (f) | الكرة الأرضيّة |
| planet | kawwkab (m) | كوّكب |
| atmosphere | el ɣelāf el gawwy (m) | الغلاف الجوّي |
| geography | goɣrafia (f) | جغرافيا |
| nature | ṭabeeʿa (f) | طبيعة |
| globe (table ~) | namūzag lel kora el arḍiya (m) | نموذج للكرة الأرضيّة |
| map | χarīṭa (f) | خريطة |
| atlas | aṭlas (m) | أطلس |
| Europe | orobba (f) | أوروبّا |
| Asia | asya (f) | آسيا |
| Africa | afreqia (f) | أفريقيا |
| Australia | ostorālya (f) | أستراليا |
| America | amrīka (f) | أمريكا |
| North America | amrīka el ʃamaliya (f) | أمريكا الشماليّة |
| South America | amrīka el ganūbiya (f) | أمريكا الجنوبيّة |
| Antarctica | el qoṭb el ganūby (m) | القطب الجنوبي |
| the Arctic | el qoṭb el ʃamāly (m) | القطب الشمالي |

## 76. Cardinal directions

| | | |
|---|---|---|
| north | ʃemāl (m) | شمال |
| to the north | lel ʃamāl | للشمال |
| in the north | fel ʃamāl | في الشمال |
| northern (adj) | ʃamāly | شمالي |
| south | ganūb (m) | جنوب |
| to the south | lel ganūb | للجنوب |
| in the south | fel ganūb | في الجنوب |
| southern (adj) | ganūby | جنوبي |
| west | ɣarb (m) | غرب |
| to the west | lel ɣarb | للغرب |
| in the west | fel ɣarb | في الغرب |
| western (adj) | ɣarby | غربي |
| east | ʃarʾ (m) | شرق |
| to the east | lel ʃarʾ | للشرق |
| in the east | fel ʃarʾ | في الشرق |
| eastern (adj) | ʃarʾy | شرقي |

## 77. Sea. Ocean

| | | |
|---|---|---|
| sea | baḥr (m) | بحر |
| ocean | moḥīṭ (m) | محيط |
| gulf (bay) | χalīg (m) | خليج |
| straits | maḍīq (m) | مضيق |
| land (solid ground) | barr (m) | برّ |
| continent (mainland) | qārra (f) | قارّة |
| island | gezīra (f) | جزيرة |
| peninsula | ʃebh gezeyra (f) | شبه جزيرة |
| archipelago | magmūʿet gozor (f) | مجموعة جزر |
| bay, cove | χalīg (m) | خليج |
| harbour | mināʾ (m) | ميناء |
| lagoon | lagūn (m) | لاجون |
| cape | raʾs (m) | رأس |
| atoll | gezīra morganiya estwaʾiya (f) | جزيرة مرجانيّة إستوائيّة |
| reef | ʃoʿāb (pl) | شعاب |
| coral | morgān (m) | مرجان |
| coral reef | ʃoʿāb morganiya (pl) | شعاب مرجانية |
| deep (adj) | ʿamīq | عميق |
| depth (deep water) | ʿomq (m) | عمق |
| abyss | el ʿomq el saḥīq (m) | العمق السحيق |
| trench (e.g. Mariana ~) | χondoq (m) | خندق |
| current (Ocean ~) | tayār (m) | تيّار |
| to surround (bathe) | ḥāṭ | حاط |
| shore | sāḥel (m) | ساحل |

| | | |
|---|---|---|
| coast | sāḥel (m) | ساحل |
| flow (flood tide) | tayār (m) | تيّار |
| ebb (ebb tide) | gozor (m) | جزر |
| shoal | meyāh ḍaḥla (f) | مياه ضحلة |
| bottom (~ of the sea) | qāʿ (m) | قاع |
| wave | mouga (f) | موجة |
| crest (~ of a wave) | qemma (f) | قمّة |
| spume (sea foam) | zabad el baḥr (m) | زبد البحر |
| storm (sea storm) | ʿāṣefa (f) | عاصفة |
| hurricane | eʿṣār (m) | إعصار |
| tsunami | tsunāmy (m) | تسونامي |
| calm (dead ~) | hodūʾ (m) | هدوء |
| quiet, calm (adj) | hady | هادئ |
| pole | ʾoṭb (m) | قطب |
| polar (adj) | ʾoṭby | قطبي |
| latitude | ʿarḍ (m) | عرض |
| longitude | χaṭṭ ṭūl (m) | خطّ طول |
| parallel | motawāz (m) | متواز |
| equator | χaṭṭ el estewāʾ (m) | خطّ الإستواء |
| sky | samāʾ (f) | سماء |
| horizon | ofoq (m) | أفق |
| air | hawāʾ (m) | هواء |
| lighthouse | manāra (f) | منارة |
| to dive (vi) | ɣāṣ | غاص |
| to sink (ab. boat) | ɣereʾ | غرق |
| treasure | konūz (pl) | كنوز |

## 78. Seas & Oceans names

| | | |
|---|---|---|
| Atlantic Ocean | el moḥeyṭ el aṭlanṭy (m) | المحيط الأطلنطي |
| Indian Ocean | el moḥeyṭ el hendy (m) | المحيط الهندي |
| Pacific Ocean | el moḥeyṭ el hādy (m) | المحيط الهادي |
| Arctic Ocean | el moḥeyṭ el motagammed el ʃamāly (m) | المحيط المتجمّد الشمالي |
| Black Sea | el baḥr el aswad (m) | البحر الأسود |
| Red Sea | el baḥr el aḥmar (m) | البحر الأحمر |
| Yellow Sea | el baḥr el aṣfar (m) | البحر الأصفر |
| White Sea | el baḥr el abyaḍ (m) | البحر الأبيض |
| Caspian Sea | baḥr qazwīn (m) | بحر قزوين |
| Dead Sea | el baḥr el mayet (m) | البحر الميّت |
| Mediterranean Sea | el baḥr el abyaḍ el motawasseṭ (m) | البحر الأبيض المتوسّط |
| Aegean Sea | baḥr eygah (m) | بحر إيجة |
| Adriatic Sea | el baḥr el adreyatīky (m) | البحر الأدرياتيكي |
| Arabian Sea | baḥr el ʿarab (m) | بحر العرب |

| | | |
|---|---|---|
| Sea of Japan | baḥr el yabān (m) | بحر اليابان |
| Bering Sea | baḥr bering (m) | بحر بيرينغ |
| South China Sea | baḥr el ṣeyn el ganūby (m) | بحر الصين الجنوبي |
| Coral Sea | baḥr el morgān (m) | بحر المرجان |
| Tasman Sea | baḥr tazman (m) | بحر تسمان |
| Caribbean Sea | el baḥr el karību (m) | البحر الكاريبي |
| Barents Sea | baḥr barents (m) | بحر بارنتس |
| Kara Sea | baḥr kara (m) | بحر كارا |
| North Sea | baḥr el ʃamāl (m) | بحر الشمال |
| Baltic Sea | baḥr el balṭīq (m) | بحر البلطيق |
| Norwegian Sea | baḥr el nerwīg (m) | بحر النرويج |

## 79. Mountains

| | | |
|---|---|---|
| mountain | gabal (m) | جبل |
| mountain range | selselet gebāl (f) | سلسلة جبال |
| mountain ridge | notū' el gabal (m) | نتوء الجبل |
| summit, top | qemma (f) | قمّة |
| peak | qemma (f) | قمّة |
| foot (~ of the mountain) | asfal (m) | أسفل |
| slope (mountainside) | monḥadar (m) | منحدر |
| volcano | borkān (m) | بركان |
| active volcano | borkān naʃeṭ (m) | بركان نشط |
| dormant volcano | borkān χāmed (m) | بركان خامد |
| eruption | sawarān (m) | ثوّران |
| crater | fawhet el borkān (f) | فوهة البركان |
| magma | magma (f) | ماجما |
| lava | ḥomam borkāniya (pl) | حمم بركانية |
| molten (~ lava) | monṣahera | منصهرة |
| canyon | wādy ḍaye' (m) | وادي ضيّق |
| gorge | mamarr ḍaye' (m) | ممرّ ضيّق |
| crevice | ʃa'' (m) | شقّ |
| abyss (chasm) | hāwya (f) | هاوية |
| pass, col | mamarr gabaly (m) | ممرّ جبلي |
| plateau | haḍaba (f) | هضبة |
| cliff | garf (m) | جرف |
| hill | tall (m) | تلّ |
| glacier | nahr galīdy (m) | نهر جليدي |
| waterfall | ʃallāl (m) | شلّال |
| geyser | nab' maya ḥāra (m) | نبع ميّة حارة |
| lake | boḥeyra (f) | بحيرة |
| plain | sahl (m) | سهل |
| landscape | manzar ṭabee'y (m) | منظر طبيعي |
| echo | ṣada (m) | صدى |

| | | |
|---|---|---|
| alpinist | motasalleq el gebāl (m) | متسلّق الجبال |
| rock climber | motasalleq ṣoχūr (m) | متسلّق صخور |
| to conquer (in climbing) | taɣallab ʿala | تغلّب على |
| climb (an easy ~) | tasalloq (m) | تسلّق |

## 80. Mountains names

| | | |
|---|---|---|
| The Alps | gebāl el alb (pl) | جبال الألب |
| Mont Blanc | mōn blōn (m) | مون بلون |
| The Pyrenees | gebāl el barānes (pl) | جبال البرانس |
| The Carpathians | gebāl el karbāt (pl) | جبال الكاربات |
| The Ural Mountains | gebāl el urāl (pl) | جبال الأورال |
| The Caucasus Mountains | gebāl el qoqāz (pl) | جبال القوقاز |
| Mount Elbrus | gabal elbrus (m) | جبل إلبروس |
| The Altai Mountains | gebāl altāy (pl) | جبال ألتاي |
| The Tian Shan | gebāl tian ʃan (pl) | جبال تيان شان |
| The Pamirs | gebāl bamir (pl) | جبال بامير |
| The Himalayas | himalāya (pl) | هيمالايا |
| Mount Everest | gabal everest (m) | جبل افرست |
| The Andes | gebāl el andīz (pl) | جبال الأنديز |
| Mount Kilimanjaro | gabal kilimanʒaro (m) | جبل كليمنجارو |

## 81. Rivers

| | | |
|---|---|---|
| river | nahr (m) | نهر |
| spring (natural source) | ʿeyn (m) | عين |
| riverbed (river channel) | magra el nahr (m) | مجرى النهر |
| basin (river valley) | ḥoḍe (m) | حوض |
| to flow into ... | ṣabb fe ... | صبّ في... |
| tributary | rāfed (m) | رافد |
| bank (river ~) | ḍaffa (f) | ضفّة |
| current (stream) | tayār (m) | تيّار |
| downstream (adv) | maʿ ettigāh magra el nahr | مع إتّجاه مجرى النهر |
| upstream (adv) | ḍed el tayār | ضد التيار |
| inundation | ɣamr (m) | غمر |
| flooding | fayaḍān (m) | فيضان |
| to overflow (vi) | fāḍ | فاض |
| to flood (vt) | ɣamar | غمر |
| shallow (shoal) | meyāh ḍaḥla (f) | مياه ضحلة |
| rapids | monḥadar el nahr (m) | منحدر النهر |
| dam | sadd (m) | سدّ |
| canal | qanah (f) | قناة |
| reservoir (artificial lake) | χazzān māʾy (m) | خزّان مائي |
| sluice, lock | bawwāba qanṭara (f) | بوّابة قنطرة |

| | | |
|---|---|---|
| water body (pond, etc.) | berka (f) | بركة |
| swamp (marshland) | mostanqa' (m) | مستنقع |
| bog, marsh | mostanqa' (m) | مستنقع |
| whirlpool | dawwāma (f) | دوّامة |
| stream (brook) | gadwal (m) | جدوّل |
| drinking (ab. water) | el ʃorb | الشرب |
| fresh (~ water) | 'azb | عذب |
| ice | galīd (m) | جليد |
| to freeze over (ab. river, etc.) | etgammed | إتجمّد |

## 82. Rivers names

| | | |
|---|---|---|
| Seine | el seyn (m) | السين |
| Loire | el lua:r (m) | اللوار |
| Thames | el teymz (m) | التيمز |
| Rhine | el rayn (m) | الراين |
| Danube | el danūb (m) | الدانوب |
| Volga | el volga (m) | الفولغا |
| Don | el done (m) | الدون |
| Lena | lena (m) | لينا |
| Yellow River | el nahr el aṣfar (m) | النهر الأصفر |
| Yangtze | el yangesty (m) | اليانغستي |
| Mekong | el mekong (m) | الميكونغ |
| Ganges | el ɣang (m) | الغانج |
| Nile River | el nīl (m) | النيل |
| Congo River | el kongo (m) | الكونغو |
| Okavango River | okavango (m) | أوكافانجو |
| Zambezi River | el zambizi (m) | الزمبيزي |
| Limpopo River | limbobo (m) | ليمبوبو |
| Mississippi River | el mississibbi (m) | الميسيسيبي |

## 83. Forest

| | | |
|---|---|---|
| forest, wood | ɣāba (f) | غابة |
| forest (as adj) | ɣāba | غابة |
| thick forest | ɣāba kasīfa (f) | غابة كثيفة |
| grove | bostān (m) | بستان |
| forest clearing | ezālet el ɣābāt (f) | إزالة الغابات |
| thicket | agama (f) | أجمة |
| scrubland | arāḍy el ʃogayrāt (pl) | أراضي الشجيرات |
| footpath (troddenpath) | mamarr (m) | ممرّ |
| gully | wādy ḍaye' (m) | وادي ضيّق |
| tree | ʃagara (f) | شجرة |

| | | |
|---|---|---|
| leaf | wara'a (f) | ورقة |
| leaves (foliage) | wara' (m) | ورق |
| fall of leaves | tasā'oṭ el awrā' (m) | تساقط الأوراق |
| to fall (ab. leaves) | saqaṭ | سقط |
| top (of the tree) | ra's (m) | رأس |
| branch | ɣoṣn (m) | غصن |
| bough | ɣoṣn ra'īsy (m) | غصن رئيسي |
| bud (on shrub, tree) | bor'om (m) | برعم |
| needle (of the pine tree) | ʃawka (f) | شوكة |
| fir cone | kūz el ṣnowbar (m) | كوز الصنوبر |
| tree hollow | gofe (m) | جوف |
| nest | 'eʃ (m) | عشّ |
| burrow (animal hole) | goḥr (m) | جحر |
| trunk | gez' (m) | جذع |
| root | gezr (m) | جذر |
| bark | leḥā' (m) | لحاء |
| moss | ṭaḥlab (m) | طحلب |
| to uproot (remove trees or tree stumps) | eqtala' | إقتلع |
| to chop down | 'aṭṭa' | قطّع |
| to deforest (vt) | azāl el ɣabāt | أزال الغابات |
| tree stump | gez' el ʃagara (m) | جذع الشجرة |
| campfire | nār moχayem (m) | نار مخيّم |
| forest fire | ḥarī' ɣāba (m) | حريق غابة |
| to extinguish (vt) | ṭaffa | طفّى |
| forest ranger | ḥāres el ɣāba (m) | حارس الغابة |
| protection | ḥemāya (f) | حماية |
| to protect (~ nature) | ḥama | حمى |
| poacher | sāre' el ṣeyd (m) | سارق الصيد |
| steel trap | maṣyada (f) | مصيّدة |
| to gather, to pick (vt) | gamma' | جمّع |
| to lose one's way | tāh | تاه |

## 84. Natural resources

| | | |
|---|---|---|
| natural resources | sarawāt ṭabī'iya (pl) | ثروات طبيعيّة |
| minerals | ma'āden (pl) | معادن |
| deposits | rawāseb (pl) | رواسب |
| field (e.g. oilfield) | ḥaql (m) | حقل |
| to mine (extract) | estaχrag | إستخرج |
| mining (extraction) | esteχrāg (m) | إستخراج |
| ore | χām (m) | خام |
| mine (e.g. for coal) | mangam (m) | منجم |
| shaft (mine ~) | mangam (m) | منجم |
| miner | 'āmel mangam (m) | عامل منجم |

| | | |
|---|---|---|
| gas (natural ~) | ɣāz (m) | غاز |
| gas pipeline | χaṭṭ anabīb ɣāz (m) | خطّ أنابيب غاز |
| oil (petroleum) | nafṭ (m) | نفط |
| oil pipeline | anabīb el nafṭ (pl) | أنابيب النفط |
| oil well | bīr el nafṭ (m) | بير النفط |
| derrick (tower) | ḥaffāra (f) | حفّارة |
| tanker | nāqelet betrūl (f) | ناقلة بترول |
| sand | raml (m) | رمل |
| limestone | ḥagar el kals (m) | حجر الكلس |
| gravel | ḥaṣa (m) | حصى |
| peat | χaθ faḥm nabāty (m) | خث فحم نباتي |
| clay | ṭīn (m) | طين |
| coal | faḥm (m) | فحم |
| iron (ore) | ḥadīd (m) | حديد |
| gold | dahab (m) | ذهب |
| silver | faḍḍa (f) | فضّة |
| nickel | nikel (m) | نيكل |
| copper | neḥās (m) | نحاس |
| zinc | zink (m) | زنك |
| manganese | manganīz (m) | منجنيز |
| mercury | ze'baq (m) | زئبق |
| lead | roṣāṣ (m) | رصاص |
| mineral | ma'dan (m) | معدن |
| crystal | kristāl (m) | كريستال |
| marble | roχām (m) | رخام |
| uranium | yuranuim (m) | يورانيوم |

## 85. Weather

| | | |
|---|---|---|
| weather | ṭa's (m) | طقس |
| weather forecast | naʃra gawiya (f) | نشرة جويّة |
| temperature | ḥarāra (f) | حرارة |
| thermometer | termometr (m) | ترمومتر |
| barometer | barometr (m) | بارومتر |
| humid (adj) | roṭob | رطب |
| humidity | roṭūba (f) | رطوبة |
| heat (extreme ~) | ḥarāra (f) | حرارة |
| hot (torrid) | ḥarr | حارّ |
| it's hot | el gaww ḥarr | الجّو حرّ |
| it's warm | el gaww dafa | الجوّ دفا |
| warm (moderately hot) | dāfe' | دافئ |
| it's cold | el gaww bāred | الجوّ بارد |
| cold (adj) | bāred | بارد |
| sun | ʃams (f) | شمس |
| to shine (vi) | nawwar | نوّر |

| | | |
|---|---|---|
| sunny (day) | moʃmes | مشمس |
| to come up (vi) | ʃara' | شرق |
| to set (vi) | ɣarab | غرب |
| cloud | saḥāba (f) | سحابة |
| cloudy (adj) | meɣayem | مغيّم |
| rain cloud | saḥābet maṭar (f) | سحابة مطر |
| somber (gloomy) | meɣayem | مغيّم |
| rain | maṭar (m) | مطر |
| it's raining | el donia betmaṭṭar | الدنيا بتمطّر |
| rainy (~ day, weather) | momṭer | ممطر |
| to drizzle (vi) | maṭṭaret razāz | مطّرت رذاذ |
| pouring rain | maṭar monhamer (f) | مطر منهمر |
| downpour | maṭar ɣazīr (m) | مطر غزير |
| heavy (e.g. ~ rain) | ʃedīd | شديد |
| puddle | berka (f) | بركة |
| to get wet (in rain) | ettbal | إتّبل |
| fog (mist) | ʃabbūra (f) | شبّورة |
| foggy | fih ʃabbūra | فيه شبّورة |
| snow | talg (m) | ثلج |
| it's snowing | fih talg | فيه ثلج |

## 86. Severe weather. Natural disasters

| | | |
|---|---|---|
| thunderstorm | ʿāṣefa raʿdiya (f) | عاصفة رعدية |
| lightning (~ strike) | bar' (m) | برق |
| to flash (vi) | baraq | برق |
| thunder | raʿd (m) | رعد |
| to thunder (vi) | dawa | دوّى |
| it's thundering | el samā' dawat raʿd (f) | السماء دوّت رعد |
| hail | maṭar bard (m) | مطر برد |
| it's hailing | maṭṭaret bard | مطّرت برد |
| to flood (vt) | ɣamar | غمر |
| flood, inundation | fayaḍān (m) | فيضان |
| earthquake | zelzāl (m) | زلزال |
| tremor, shoke | hazza arḍiya (f) | هزّة أرضية |
| epicentre | markaz el zelzāl (m) | مركز الزلزال |
| eruption | sawarān (m) | ثوّران |
| lava | ḥomam borkāniya (pl) | حمم بركانية |
| twister, tornado | eʿṣār (m) | إعصار |
| typhoon | tyfūn (m) | طوفان |
| hurricane | eʿṣār (m) | إعصار |
| storm | ʿāṣefa (f) | عاصفة |
| tsunami | tsunāmy (m) | تسونامي |

| | | |
|---|---|---|
| cyclone | eʿṣār (m) | إعصار |
| bad weather | ṭaʾs sayeʾ (m) | طقس سئ |
| fire (accident) | ḥarīʾ (m) | حريق |
| disaster | karsa (f) | كارثة |
| meteorite | nayzek (m) | نيّزك |
| | | |
| avalanche | enheyār talgy (m) | إنهيار ثلجي |
| snowslide | enheyār talgy (m) | إنهيار ثلجي |
| blizzard | ʿāṣefa talgiya (f) | عاصفة ثلجيّة |
| snowstorm | ʿāṣefa talgiya (f) | عاصفة ثلجيّة |

# FAUNA

## 87. Mammals. Predators

| | | |
|---|---|---|
| predator | moftares (m) | مفترس |
| tiger | nemr (m) | نمر |
| lion | asad (m) | أسد |
| wolf | ze'b (m) | ذئب |
| fox | ta'lab (m) | ثعلب |
| jaguar | nemr amrīky (m) | نمر أمريكي |
| leopard | fahd (m) | فهد |
| cheetah | fahd ṣayād (m) | فهد صيّاد |
| black panther | nemr aswad (m) | نمر أسوّد |
| puma | asad el gebāl (m) | أسد الجبال |
| snow leopard | nemr el tolūg (m) | نمر الثلوج |
| lynx | waʃaq (m) | وشق |
| coyote | qayūṭ (m) | قيوط |
| jackal | ebn 'āwy (m) | ابن آوى |
| hyena | ḍeb' (m) | ضبع |

## 88. Wild animals

| | | |
|---|---|---|
| animal | ḥayawān (m) | حيوان |
| beast (animal) | waḥʃ (m) | وحش |
| squirrel | sengāb (m) | سنجاب |
| hedgehog | qonfoz (m) | قنفذ |
| hare | arnab barry (m) | أرنب برّي |
| rabbit | arnab (m) | أرنب |
| badger | ɣarīr (m) | غرير |
| raccoon | rakūn (m) | راكون |
| hamster | hamster (m) | هامستر |
| marmot | marmoṭ (m) | مرموط |
| mole | χold (m) | خلد |
| mouse | fār (m) | فأر |
| rat | gerz (m) | جرذ |
| bat | χoffāʃ (m) | خفّاش |
| ermine | qāqem (m) | قاقم |
| sable | sammūr (m) | سمّور |
| marten | fara'īāt (m) | فرائيات |
| weasel | ebn 'ers (m) | ابن عرس |
| mink | mink (m) | منك |

| | | |
|---|---|---|
| beaver | qondos (m) | قندس |
| otter | ta'lab maya (m) | ثعلب الميّة |
| | | |
| horse | ḥoṣān (m) | حصان |
| moose | eyl el mūz (m) | أيّل الموظ |
| deer | ayl (m) | أيل |
| camel | gamal (m) | جمل |
| | | |
| bison | bison (m) | بيسون |
| wisent | byson orobby (m) | بيسون أوروبي |
| buffalo | gamūs (m) | جاموس |
| | | |
| zebra | ḥomār waḥʃy (m) | حمار وحشي |
| antelope | ẓaby (m) | ظبي |
| roe deer | yaḥmūr orobby (m) | يحمورأوروبي |
| fallow deer | eyl asmar orobby (m) | أيّل أسمر أوروبي |
| chamois | ʃamwah (f) | شاموا ه |
| wild boar | χenzīr barry (m) | خنزير برّي |
| | | |
| whale | ḥūt (m) | حوت |
| seal | foqma (f) | فقمة |
| walrus | el kab' (m) | الكبع |
| fur seal | foqmet el farā' (f) | فقمة الفراء |
| dolphin | dolfīn (m) | دولفين |
| | | |
| bear | dobb (m) | دبّ |
| polar bear | dobb 'oṭṭby (m) | دبّ قطبي |
| panda | banda (m) | باندا |
| | | |
| monkey | 'erd (m) | قرد |
| chimpanzee | ʃimbanzy (m) | شيمبانزي |
| orangutan | orangutan (m) | أورنغوتان |
| gorilla | ɣorella (f) | غوريلا |
| macaque | 'erd el makāk (m) | قرد المكاك |
| gibbon | gibbon (m) | جيبون |
| | | |
| elephant | fīl (m) | فيل |
| rhinoceros | χartīt (m) | خرتيت |
| giraffe | zarāfa (f) | زرافة |
| hippopotamus | faras el nahr (m) | فرس النهر |
| | | |
| kangaroo | kangarū (m) | كانجّارو |
| koala (bear) | el koala (m) | الكوالا |
| | | |
| mongoose | nems (m) | نمس |
| chinchilla | ʃenʃīla (f) | شنشيلة |
| skunk | ẓerbān (m) | ظربان |
| porcupine | nīṣ (m) | نيص |

## 89. Domestic animals

| | | |
|---|---|---|
| cat | 'oṭṭa (f) | قطّة |
| tomcat | 'oṭṭ (m) | قطّ |
| dog | kalb (m) | كلب |

| | | |
|---|---|---|
| horse | ḥoṣān (m) | حصان |
| stallion (male horse) | χeyl faḥl (m) | خيل فحل |
| mare | faras (f) | فرس |
| cow | ba'ara (f) | بقرة |
| bull | sore (m) | ثور |
| ox | sore (m) | ثور |
| sheep (ewe) | χarūf (f) | خروف |
| ram | kebʃ (m) | كبش |
| goat | me'za (f) | معزة |
| billy goat, he-goat | mā'ez zakar (m) | ماعز ذكر |
| donkey | ḥomār (m) | حمار |
| mule | baɣl (m) | بغل |
| pig | χenzīr (m) | خنزير |
| piglet | χannūṣ (m) | خنّوص |
| rabbit | arnab (m) | أرنب |
| hen (chicken) | farχa (f) | فرخة |
| cock | dīk (m) | ديك |
| duck | baṭṭa (f) | بطّة |
| drake | dakar el baṭṭ (m) | ذكر البط |
| goose | wezza (f) | وزّة |
| tom turkey, gobbler | dīk rūmy (m) | ديك رومي |
| turkey (hen) | dīk rūmy (m) | ديك رومي |
| domestic animals | ḥayawānāt dawāgen (pl) | حيوانات دواجن |
| tame (e.g. ~ hamster) | alīf | أليف |
| to tame (vt) | rawweḍ | روّض |
| to breed (vt) | rabba | ربى |
| farm | mazra'a (f) | مزرعة |
| poultry | dawāgen (pl) | دواجن |
| cattle | māʃeya (f) | ماشية |
| herd (cattle) | qaṭee' (m) | قطيع |
| stable | esṭabl χeyl (m) | إسطبل خيل |
| pigsty | ḥazīret χanazīr (f) | حظيرة الخنازير |
| cowshed | zerībet el ba'ar (f) | زريبة البقر |
| rabbit hutch | qan el arāneb (m) | قن الأرانب |
| hen house | qan el ferāχ (m) | قن الفراخ |

## 90. Birds

| | | |
|---|---|---|
| bird | ṭā'er (m) | طائر |
| pigeon | ḥamāma (f) | حمامة |
| sparrow | 'aṣfūr dawri (m) | عصفور دوري |
| tit (great tit) | qarqaf (m) | قرقف |
| magpie | 'a''a' (m) | عقعق |
| raven | ɣorāb aswad (m) | غراب أسود |

| | | |
|---|---|---|
| crow | ɣorāb (m) | غراب |
| jackdaw | zāɣ zarʿy (m) | زاغ زرعي |
| rook | ɣorāb el qeyẓ (m) | غراب القيظ |
| | | |
| duck | baṭṭa (f) | بطّة |
| goose | wezza (f) | وزّة |
| pheasant | tadarrog (m) | تدرج |
| | | |
| eagle | ʿeqāb (m) | عقاب |
| hawk | el bāz (m) | الباز |
| falcon | ṣaʾr (m) | صقر |
| vulture | nesr (m) | نسر |
| condor (Andean ~) | kondor (m) | كندور |
| | | |
| swan | el temm (m) | التمّ |
| crane | karkiya (m) | كركية |
| stork | loqloq (m) | لقلق |
| | | |
| parrot | babaɣāʾ (m) | ببغاء |
| hummingbird | ṭannān (m) | طنّان |
| peacock | ṭawūs (m) | طاووس |
| | | |
| ostrich | naʿāma (f) | نعامة |
| heron | belʃone (m) | بلشون |
| flamingo | flamingo (m) | فلامينجو |
| pelican | bagʿa (f) | بجعة |
| | | |
| nightingale | ʿandalīb (m) | عندليب |
| swallow | el sonūnū (m) | السنونو |
| | | |
| thrush | somnet el ḥoqūl (m) | سمنة الحقول |
| song thrush | somna moɣarreda (m) | سمنة مغرّدة |
| blackbird | ʃaḥrūr aswad (m) | شحرور أسود |
| | | |
| swift | semmāma (m) | سمّامة |
| lark | qabra (f) | قبرة |
| quail | semmān (m) | سمّان |
| | | |
| woodpecker | naʾār el χaʃab (m) | نقار الخشب |
| cuckoo | weqwāq (m) | وقواق |
| owl | būma (f) | بومة |
| eagle owl | būm orāsy (m) | بوم أوراسي |
| wood grouse | dīk el χalang (m) | ديك الخلنج |
| black grouse | ṭyhūg aswad (m) | طيهوج أسوّد |
| partridge | el ḥagal (m) | الحجل |
| | | |
| starling | zerzūr (m) | زرزور |
| canary | kanāry (m) | كناري |
| hazel grouse | ṭyhūg el bondoʾ (m) | طيهوج البندق |
| | | |
| chaffinch | ʃarʃūr (m) | شرشور |
| bullfinch | deɣnāʃ (m) | دغناش |
| | | |
| seagull | nawras (m) | نورس |
| albatross | el qoṭros (m) | القطرس |
| penguin | beṭrīq (m) | بطريق |

## 91. Fish. Marine animals

| | | |
|---|---|---|
| bream | abramīs (m) | أبراميس |
| carp | ʃabbūṭ (m) | شبّوط |
| perch | farχ (m) | فرخ |
| catfish | 'armūṭ (m) | قرموط |
| pike | karāky (m) | كراكي |
| salmon | salamon (m) | سلمون |
| sturgeon | ḥafʃ (m) | حفش |
| herring | renga (f) | رنجة |
| Atlantic salmon | salamon aṭlasy (m) | سلمون أطلسي |
| mackerel | makerel (m) | ماكريل |
| flatfish | samak mefalṭah (f) | سمك مفلطح |
| zander, pike perch | samak sandar (m) | سمك سندر |
| cod | el qadd (m) | القد |
| tuna | tuna (f) | تونة |
| trout | salamon mera''aṭ (m) | سلمون مرقّط |
| eel | ḥankalīs (m) | حنكليس |
| electric ray | ra'ād (m) | رعاد |
| moray eel | moraya (f) | مورايية |
| piranha | bīrana (f) | بيرانا |
| shark | 'erʃ (m) | قرش |
| dolphin | dolfīn (m) | دولفين |
| whale | ḥūt (m) | حوت |
| crab | kaboria (m) | كابوريا |
| jellyfish | 'andīl el baḥr (m) | قنديل البحر |
| octopus | aχṭabūṭ (m) | أخطبوط |
| starfish | negmet el baḥr (f) | نجمة البحر |
| sea urchin | qonfoz el baḥr (m) | قنفذ البحر |
| seahorse | ḥoṣān el baḥr (m) | حصان البحر |
| oyster | mahār (m) | محار |
| prawn | gammbary (m) | جمّبري |
| lobster | estakoza (f) | استكوزا |
| spiny lobster | estakoza (m) | استاكوزا |

## 92. Amphibians. Reptiles

| | | |
|---|---|---|
| snake | te'bān (m) | ثعبان |
| venomous (snake) | sām | سام |
| viper | af'a (f) | أفعى |
| cobra | kobra (m) | كوبرا |
| python | te'bān byton (m) | ثعبان بايثون |
| boa | bawā' el 'aṣera (f) | بواء العاصرة |
| grass snake | te'bān el 'oʃb (m) | ثعبان العشب |

| | | |
|---|---|---|
| rattle snake | af'a megalgela (f) | أفعى مجلجلة |
| anaconda | anakonda (f) | أناكوندا |
| lizard | seḥliya (f) | سحليّة |
| iguana | eɣwana (f) | إغوانة |
| monitor lizard | warl (m) | ورل |
| salamander | salamander (m) | سلمندر |
| chameleon | ḥerbāya (f) | حرباية |
| scorpion | 'a'rab (m) | عقرب |
| turtle | solḥefah (f) | سلحفاة |
| frog | ḍeffḍa' (m) | ضفدع |
| toad | ḍeffḍa' el ṭeyn (m) | ضفدع الطين |
| crocodile | temsāḥ (m) | تمساح |

## 93. Insects

| | | |
|---|---|---|
| insect | ḥaʃara (f) | حشرة |
| butterfly | farāʃa (f) | فراشة |
| ant | namla (f) | نملة |
| fly | debbāna (f) | دبّانة |
| mosquito | namūsa (f) | ناموسة |
| beetle | χonfesa (f) | خنفسة |
| wasp | dabbūr (m) | دبّور |
| bee | naḥla (f) | نحلة |
| bumblebee | naḥla ṭannāna (f) | نحلة طنّانة |
| gadfly (botfly) | na'ra (f) | نعرة |
| spider | 'ankabūt (m) | عنكبوت |
| spider's web | nasīg 'ankabūt (m) | نسيج عنكبوت |
| dragonfly | ya'sūb (m) | يعسوب |
| grasshopper | garād (m) | جراد |
| moth (night butterfly) | 'etta (f) | عثّة |
| cockroach | ṣarṣūr (m) | صرصور |
| tick | qarāda (f) | قرادة |
| flea | barɣūt (m) | برغوث |
| midge | ba'ūḍa (f) | بعوضة |
| locust | garād (m) | جراد |
| snail | ḥalazōn (m) | حلزون |
| cricket | ṣarṣūr el ḥaql (m) | صرصور الحقل |
| firefly | yarā'a (f) | يراعة |
| ladybird | χonfesa mena'ṭṭa (f) | خنفسة منقّطة |
| cockchafer | χonfesa motlefa lel nabāt (f) | خنفسة متلفة للنبات |
| leech | 'alaqa (f) | علقة |
| caterpillar | yasrū' (m) | يسروع |
| earthworm | dūda (f) | دودة |
| larva | yaraqa (f) | يرقة |

# FLORA

## 94. Trees

| | | |
|---|---|---|
| tree | ʃagara (f) | شجرة |
| deciduous (adj) | nafḍiya | نفضيّة |
| coniferous (adj) | ṣonoberiya | صنوبرية |
| evergreen (adj) | dā'emet el χoḍra | دائمة الخضرة |
| apple tree | ʃagaret toffāḥ (f) | شجرة تفّاح |
| pear tree | ʃagaret komettra (f) | شجرة كمثّرى |
| cherry tree | ʃagaret karaz (f) | شجرة كرز |
| plum tree | ʃagaret bar'ū' (f) | شجرة برقوق |
| birch | batola (f) | بتولا |
| oak | ballūṭ (f) | بلّوط |
| linden tree | zayzafūn (f) | زيزفون |
| aspen | ḥūr rāgef | حور راجف |
| maple | qayqab (f) | قيقب |
| spruce | rateng (f) | راتينج |
| pine | ṣonober (f) | صنوبر |
| larch | arziya (f) | أرزية |
| fir tree | tanūb (f) | تنوب |
| cedar | el orz (f) | الأرز |
| poplar | ḥūr (f) | حور |
| rowan | ɣobayrā' (f) | غبيراء |
| willow | ṣefsāf (f) | صفصاف |
| alder | gār el mā' (m) | جار الماء |
| beech | el zān (f) | الزان |
| elm | derdar (f) | دردار |
| ash (tree) | marān (f) | مران |
| chestnut | kastanā' (f) | كستناء |
| magnolia | maɣnolia (f) | ماغنوليا |
| palm tree | naχla (f) | نخلة |
| cypress | el soro (f) | السرو |
| mangrove | mangrūf (f) | مانجروف |
| baobab | baobab (f) | باوباب |
| eucalyptus | eukalyptus (f) | أوكالبتوس |
| sequoia | sequoia (f) | سيكويا |

## 95. Shrubs

| | | |
|---|---|---|
| bush | ʃogeyra (f) | شجيرة |
| shrub | ʃogayrāt (pl) | شجيرات |

| | | |
|---|---|---|
| grapevine | karma (f) | كرمة |
| vineyard | karam (m) | كرم |
| raspberry bush | zarʿet tūt el ʿalīʾ el aḥmar (f) | زرعة توت العليق الأحمر |
| redcurrant bush | keʃmeʃ aḥmar (m) | كشمش أحمر |
| gooseberry bush | ʿenab el saʿlab (m) | عنب الثعلب |
| acacia | aqaqia (f) | أقاقيا |
| barberry | berbarīs (m) | برباريس |
| jasmine | yasmīn (m) | ياسمين |
| juniper | ʿarʿar (m) | عرعر |
| rosebush | ʃogeyret ward (f) | شجيرة ورد |
| dog rose | ward el seyāg (pl) | ورد السياج |

## 96. Fruits. Berries

| | | |
|---|---|---|
| fruit | tamra (f) | تمرة |
| fruits | tamr (m) | تمر |
| apple | toffāḥa (f) | تفّاحة |
| pear | komettra (f) | كمّثرى |
| plum | barʾūʾ (m) | برقوق |
| strawberry (garden ~) | farawla (f) | فراولة |
| cherry | karaz (m) | كرز |
| grape | ʿenab (m) | عنب |
| raspberry | tūt el ʿalīʾ el aḥmar (m) | توت العليق الأحمر |
| blackcurrant | keʃmeʃ aswad (m) | كشمش أسود |
| redcurrant | keʃmeʃ aḥmar (m) | كشمش أحمر |
| gooseberry | ʿenab el saʿlab (m) | عنب الثعلب |
| cranberry | ʿenabiya ḥāda el χebāʾ (m) | عنبية حادة الخباء |
| orange | bortoqāl (m) | برتقال |
| tangerine | yosfy (m) | يوسفي |
| pineapple | ananās (m) | أناناس |
| banana | moze (m) | موز |
| date | tamr (m) | تمر |
| lemon | lymūn (m) | ليمون |
| apricot | meʃmeʃ (f) | مشمش |
| peach | χawχa (f) | خوخة |
| kiwi | kiwi (m) | كيوي |
| grapefruit | grabe frūt (m) | جريب فروت |
| berry | tūt (m) | توت |
| berries | tūt (pl) | توت |
| cowberry | ʿenab el sore (m) | عنب الثور |
| wild strawberry | farawla barriya (f) | فراولة بريّة |
| bilberry | ʿenab al aḥrāg (m) | عنب الأحراج |

## 97. Flowers. Plants

| | | |
|---|---|---|
| flower | zahra (f) | زهرة |
| bouquet (of flowers) | bokeyh (f) | بوكيه |
| rose (flower) | warda (f) | وردة |
| tulip | tolīb (f) | توليب |
| carnation | 'oronfol (m) | قرنفل |
| gladiolus | el dalbūs (f) | الدَلَبُوث |
| cornflower | qanṭeryūn ʻanbary (m) | قنطريون عنبري |
| harebell | garīs mostadīr el awrā' (m) | جريس مستدير الأوراق |
| dandelion | handabā' (f) | هندباء |
| camomile | kamomile (f) | كاموميل |
| aloe | el alowa (m) | الألوّة |
| cactus | ṣabbār (m) | صبّار |
| rubber plant, ficus | faykas (m) | فيكس |
| lily | zanbaq (f) | زنبق |
| geranium | ɣarnūqy (f) | غرنوقي |
| hyacinth | el lavender (f) | اللافندر |
| mimosa | mimoza (f) | ميموزا |
| narcissus | nerges (f) | نرجس |
| nasturtium | abo χangar (f) | أبو خنجر |
| orchid | orkid (f) | أوركيد |
| peony | fawnia (f) | فاوانيا |
| violet | el banafseg (f) | البنفسج |
| pansy | bansy (f) | بانسي |
| forget-me-not | 'āzān el fa'r (pl) | آذان الفأر |
| daisy | aqwaḥān (f) | أقحوان |
| poppy | el χoʃχāʃ (f) | الخشخاش |
| hemp | qanb (m) | قنب |
| mint | neʻnāʻ (m) | نعناع |
| lily of the valley | zanbaq el wādy (f) | زنبق الوادي |
| snowdrop | zahrat el laban (f) | زهرة اللبن |
| nettle | 'arrāṣ (m) | قرّاص |
| sorrel | ḥammāḍ bostāny (m) | حمّاض بستاني |
| water lily | niloferiya (f) | نيلوفرية |
| fern | sarχas (m) | سرخس |
| lichen | aʃna (f) | أشنة |
| conservatory (greenhouse) | ṣoba (f) | صوبة |
| lawn | ʻoʃb aχḍar (m) | عشب أخضر |
| flowerbed | geneynet zohūr (f) | جنينة زهور |
| plant | nabāt (m) | نبات |
| grass | ʻoʃb (m) | عشب |
| blade of grass | ʻoʃba (f) | عشبة |

| | | |
|---|---|---|
| leaf | wara'a (f) | ورقة |
| petal | wara'et el zahra (f) | ورقة الزهرة |
| stem | sāq (f) | ساق |
| tuber | darna (f) | درنة |
| young plant (shoot) | nabta saɣīra (f) | نبتة صغيرة |
| thorn | ʃawka (f) | شوكة |
| to blossom (vi) | fattaḥet | فتّحت |
| to fade, to wither | debel | ذبل |
| smell (odour) | rīḥa (f) | ريحة |
| to cut (flowers) | 'aṭa' | قطع |
| to pick (a flower) | 'aṭaf | قطف |

## 98. Cereals, grains

| | | |
|---|---|---|
| grain | ḥobūb (pl) | حبوب |
| cereal crops | maḥaṣīl el ḥubūb (pl) | محاصيل الحبوب |
| ear (of barley, etc.) | sonbola (f) | سنبلة |
| wheat | 'amḥ (m) | قمح |
| rye | ʃelm mazrū' (m) | شيلم مزروع |
| oats | ʃofān (m) | شوفان |
| millet | el deχn (m) | الدُخن |
| barley | ʃe'īr (m) | شعير |
| maize | dora (f) | ذرة |
| rice | rozz (m) | رزّ |
| buckwheat | ḥanṭa soda' (f) | حنطة سوداء |
| pea plant | besella (f) | بسلّة |
| kidney bean | faṣolya (f) | فاصوليا |
| soya | fūl el ṣoya (m) | فول الصويا |
| lentil | 'ads (m) | عدس |
| beans (pulse crops) | fūl (m) | فول |

# COUNTRIES OF THE WORLD

## 99. Countries. Part 1

| | | |
|---|---|---|
| Afghanistan | afɣanistan (f) | أفغانستان |
| Albania | albānia (f) | ألبانيا |
| Argentina | arʒantīn (f) | الأرجنتين |
| Armenia | armīnia (f) | أرمينيا |
| Australia | ostorālya (f) | أستراليا |
| Austria | el nemsa (f) | النمسا |
| Azerbaijan | azrabiʒān (m) | أذربيجان |
| The Bahamas | gozor el bahāmas (pl) | جزر البهاماس |
| Bangladesh | bangladeʃ (f) | بنجلاديش |
| Belarus | belarūsia (f) | بيلاروسيا |
| Belgium | balʒīka (f) | بلجيكا |
| Bolivia | bolivia (f) | بوليفيا |
| Bosnia and Herzegovina | el bosna wel harsek (f) | البوسنة والهرسك |
| Brazil | el barazīl (f) | البرازيل |
| Bulgaria | bolɣāria (f) | بلغاريا |
| Cambodia | kambodya (f) | كمبوديا |
| Canada | kanada (f) | كندا |
| Chile | tʃīly (f) | تشيلي |
| China | el ṣīn (f) | الصين |
| Colombia | kolombia (f) | كولومبيا |
| Croatia | kroātya (f) | كرواتيا |
| Cuba | kūba (f) | كوبا |
| Cyprus | 'obroṣ (f) | قبرص |
| Czech Republic | gomhoriya el tʃīk (f) | جمهورية التشيك |
| Denmark | el denmark (f) | الدنمارك |
| Dominican Republic | gomhoriya el dominikan (f) | جمهوريّة الدومينيكان |
| Ecuador | el equador (f) | الإكوادور |
| Egypt | maṣr (f) | مصر |
| England | engeltera (f) | إنجلترا |
| Estonia | estūnia (f) | إستونيا |
| Finland | finlanda (f) | فنلندا |
| France | faransa (f) | فرنسا |
| French Polynesia | bolenezia el faransiya (f) | بولينزيا الفرنسيّة |
| Georgia | ʒorʒia (f) | جورجيا |
| Germany | almānya (f) | ألمانيا |
| Ghana | ɣana (f) | غانا |
| Great Britain | briṭaniya el 'ozma (f) | بريطانيا العظمى |
| Greece | el yunān (f) | اليونان |
| Haiti | haīti (f) | هايتي |
| Hungary | el magar (f) | المجر |

## 100. Countries. Part 2

| | | |
|---|---|---|
| Iceland | 'āyslanda (f) | آيسلندا |
| India | el hend (f) | الهند |
| Indonesia | indonisya (f) | إندونيسيا |
| Iran | iran (f) | إيران |
| Iraq | el 'erāq (m) | العراق |
| Ireland | irelanda (f) | أيرلندا |
| Israel | isra'īl (f) | إسرائيل |
| Italy | eṭālia (f) | إيطاليا |
| Jamaica | ʒamayka (f) | جامايكا |
| Japan | el yabān (f) | اليابان |
| Jordan | el ordon (m) | الأردن |
| Kazakhstan | kazaχistān (f) | كازاخستّان |
| Kenya | kenya (f) | كينيا |
| Kirghizia | qirɣizestān (f) | قيرغيزستان |
| Kuwait | el kuweyt (f) | الكويت |
| Laos | laos (f) | لاوس |
| Latvia | latvia (f) | لاتفيا |
| Lebanon | lebnān (f) | لبنان |
| Libya | libya (f) | ليبيا |
| Liechtenstein | liʃtenʃtayn (m) | ليشتنشتاين |
| Lithuania | litwānia (f) | ليتوانيا |
| Luxembourg | luksemburg (f) | لوكسمبورج |
| North Macedonia | maqdūnia (f) | مقدونيا |
| Madagascar | madaɣaʃkar (f) | مدغشقر |
| Malaysia | malīzya (f) | ماليزيا |
| Malta | malṭa (f) | مالطا |
| Mexico | el maksīk (f) | المكسيك |
| Moldova, Moldavia | moldāvia (f) | مولدافيا |
| Monaco | monako (f) | موناكو |
| Mongolia | manɣūlia (f) | منغوليا |
| Montenegro | el gabal el aswad (m) | الجبل الأسوّد |
| Morocco | el maɣreb (m) | المغرب |
| Myanmar | myanmar (f) | ميانمار |
| Namibia | namibia (f) | ناميبيا |
| Nepal | nebāl (f) | نيبال |
| Netherlands | holanda (f) | هولندا |
| New Zealand | nyu zelanda (f) | نيوزيلنّدا |
| North Korea | korea el ʃamāliya (f) | كوريا الشماليّة |
| Norway | el nerwīg (f) | النرويج |

## 101. Countries. Part 3

| | | |
|---|---|---|
| Pakistan | bakistān (f) | باكستان |
| Palestine | felesṭīn (f) | فلسطين |
| Panama | banama (f) | بنما |
| Paraguay | baraguay (f) | باراجواي |

| | | |
|---|---|---|
| Peru | beru (f) | بيرو |
| Poland | bolanda (f) | بولّندا |
| Portugal | el bortoɣāl (f) | البرتغال |
| Romania | romānia (f) | رومانيا |
| Russia | rūsya (f) | روسيا |
| Saudi Arabia | el so'odiya (f) | السعوديّة |
| Scotland | oskotlanda (f) | اسكتّلندا |
| Senegal | el senɣāl (f) | السنغال |
| Serbia | ṣerbia (f) | صربيا |
| Slovakia | slovākia (f) | سلوفاكيا |
| Slovenia | slovenia (f) | سلوفينيا |
| South Africa | afreqia el ganūbiya (f) | أفريقيا الجنوبيّة |
| South Korea | korea el ganūbiya (f) | كوريا الجنوبيّة |
| Spain | asbānya (f) | إسبانيا |
| Suriname | surinam (f) | سورينام |
| Sweden | el sweyd (f) | السويد |
| Switzerland | swesra (f) | سويسرا |
| Syria | soria (f) | سوريا |
| Taiwan | taywān (f) | تايوان |
| Tajikistan | ṭaʒīkistan (f) | طاجيكستان |
| Tanzania | tanznia (f) | تنزانيا |
| Tasmania | tasmania (f) | تاسمانيا |
| Thailand | tayland (f) | تايلاند |
| Tunisia | tunis (f) | تونس |
| Turkey | turkia (f) | تركيا |
| Turkmenistan | turkmānistān (f) | تركمانستان |
| Ukraine | okrānia (f) | أوكرانيا |
| United Arab Emirates | el emārāt el 'arabiya el mottaḥeda (pl) | الإمارات العربية المتّحدة |
| United States of America | el welayāt el mottaḥda el amrīkiya (pl) | الولايات المتّحدة الأمريكيّة |
| Uruguay | uruguay (f) | أوروجواي |
| Uzbekistan | uzbakistān (f) | أوزبكستان |
| Vatican City | el vatikān (m) | الفاتيكان |
| Venezuela | venzweyla (f) | فنزويلا |
| Vietnam | vietnām (f) | فيتنام |
| Zanzibar | zanʒibār (f) | زنجبار |

www.ingramcontent.com/pod-product-compliance
Lightning Source LLC
Chambersburg PA
CBHW070822050426
42452CB00011B/2150
* 9 7 8 1 7 8 7 1 6 7 1 7 9 *